HOW TO
TRAIN YOUR DOG
IN
SIX WEEKS

HOW TO
TRAIN YOUR DOG
IN
SIX WEEKS

BY

BILL LANDESMAN

AND

KATHLEEN BERMAN

Illustrated

A World of Books That Fill a Need

FREDERICK FELL PUBLISHERS, INC. NEW YORK

Library of Congress Cataloging in Publication Data

Landesman, Bill.
  How to train your dog in six weeks.

  SUMMARY: A guide to training a dog, selecting the
right breed, teaching him tricks, and attending to his
feeding, health, and grooming.
    1. Dogs--Training--Juvenile literature. [1. Dogs--
Training] I. Berman, Kathleen, joint author. II. Ti-
tle.
SF431.L36   636.7   75-45459
ISBN 0-8119-0266-8

For information address:
Frederick Fell Publishers, Inc.
386 Park Avenue South
New York, N.Y. 10016

Published simultaneously in Canada by
George J. McLeod, Limited, Toronto 2B, Ontario

MANUFACTURED IN THE UNITED STATES OF AMERICA

Acknowledgement

The authors wish to thank Charles Berman for his photographic excellence and his expertise in capturing shots that set this book far apart from most. Through his skills the reader is afforded maximum visual guidance, thus providing a superbly accurate supplementation of the written text.

We also wish to give mention to Dream (Landesman), Flirt (Berman), and Tippy (Fasullo) for contributing the modeling services that are an essential component of this book.

And thanks to Arlene and Karen whose patience helped the success of the venture.

With special thanks to Fritz, who made this book possible.

Contents

HOW TO
TRAIN YOUR DOG
IN
SIX WEEKS

What kind of dog for you and your family?

Choosing a puppy is always a joyful experience, but, if tempered with good judgment, the transient joy will become a lasting pleasure for all concerned. The noblest treasure you can receive from your dog is an abiding love that lifts you from the mundane, indifferent, hostile world to an echelon of value, self-esteem, and primal worth otherwise hard to come by in this life. As with love, there is mutual responsibility, and it is for the enrichment of your union that you convey the boundaries that will nurture fulfillment and a lifetime of happiness for both of you.

Now that you have been flushed with the poetry of purpose, we must become practical. If you are unable to walk your dog, for any reason, on a regular basis, or if it is impractical for you to be saddled to the daily routine of his elimination outside of the home, then perhaps you should consider a dog that can be completely paper trained. It is unusual, and often confusing to a dog, to expect him to relieve himself on paper sometimes and eliminate outside on other occasions. The choice should be made by you beforehand as to whether your pup will be paper trained or housebroken. As we will see throughout the entire training procedure, consistency is the single most important element in conveying to your pet what is expected of him and in defining the boundaries of behavior beyond which you will not allow him to transgress.

Assuming that your decision is to paper train your dog, you will find one of the smaller breeds preferable. A paper-trained St. Bernard or Great Dane might strain an otherwise amicable relationship between you and your garbage man, unless you could train the dog to flush his own waste down the toilet.

Among the smaller breeds you must further select one that will not chew your household possessions into excelsior. Many dogs, when left alone, make a vocation of chewing everything accessible, not from spite, as most people allow themselves to believe, but from anxiety. All dogs have anxiety as to whether their masters will return, but those with the greatest apprehension make the most omnivorous chewers.

A breed such as the toy poodle or Shetland sheepdog will produce a

11

diminutive stool and will not be excessively anxious when left alone. When we mention chewing, we are not including pups up to six months of age. All puppies chew. This is perfectly normal because they are teething. Beyond six months old, when your dog has passed from naivete into the age of reason, you may define whether he is a chronic masticator.

If you are unable to walk your dog and refuse to have him paper trained, then the only alternative is to have him eliminate in a confined area in your yard. Do not let the dog off the leash in the street, rationalizing that your responsibility ends with swinging the front door open. Not only is this unlawful, but you are just around the corner from a very dead dog. Having a pet is a commitment of responsibility to another living creature, and, since a dog is totally dependent upon you for his welfare, you should enter the relationship with sober commitment to the task at hand. Anyone who can't or won't abide by the aforementioned alternatives, should not have a dog. A cat or bird can be a sane compromise in that situation.

If you have children or a very busy household, you need a dog that is not inordinately high strung. A good candidate would be a big, calm, steady dog, one that might have to take physical punishment and abuse from children. An example of a big dog that can take abuse from children without getting hurt or becoming aggressive would be a Great Dane, St. Bernard, or Great Pyrenees. If your dog is going to be left alone for long periods of time during the day, you would not want to get one of the hunting breeds. A similarly bad choice would be some of the northern breeds. They can all be notoriously heavy chewers. For this reason, again, you should probably opt for one of the calmer breeds just mentioned, or a more moderate-size dog such as a good shepherd or a Doberman.

If the dog is not going to be left alone all day, and you have children, then you'll want a friendly, docile, sweet dog. You could consider one of the hunting breeds or a good German shepherd. What you want to avoid, with a lot of children, is a small dog like a toy poodle, schnauzer, or Chihuahua that is going to have to defend himself against pinching, poking, and pulling little hands. These dogs realize their precarious safety and are quick to retaliate by nipping and biting. Such a situation is torture for the dog and dangerous for the child.

As far as obedience training for competition, or to achieve competence on a working-dog level, a poor choice would be an Afghan or a northern breed of dog such as a Siberian husky, malamute, or chow chow. These dogs have little desire to please, although they are not stupid.

GUARD WORK:
BITE AND
RELEASE
ON COMMAND

WHO SAID A
GUARD DOG
CAN'T BE LOVABLE?

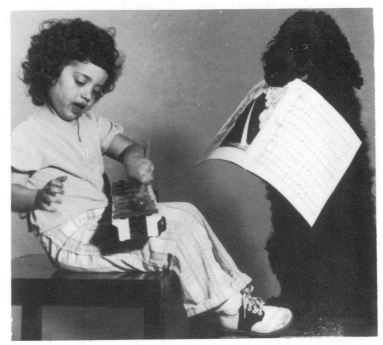

A dog that is not motivated by a strong love for his owners and a compelling desire to please will never achieve anything but the most preliminary refinements of basic obedience. If obedience is enforced with consistency, your dog will at least be livable; and if you don't require too much from him, he should be somewhat lovable. A dog can and should be so much more than a manure machine or the latest fad. Most owners don't realize how much their dog is capable of or how smart it really is. Only with proper training can you reaize your animal's full potential and set up an even closer bond of mutual love and respect.

A dog such as the standard poodle would be very good for competition and can achieve the highest level of obedience possible, as can a good Doberman or shepherd. Not only are they highly intelligent, but the desire to please is so great that these dogs can realize the zenith of their capabilities in a surprisingly short time, with skillful training. When I say a good dog, I mean one that is not nervous, aggressive, or shy, and does not have any of the numerous negative characteristics that are found through indiscriminate inbreeding in the puppy mills. Assembly-line dogs find their way into your local pet shops and then into your heart. At that point the trouble is just beginning. We will discuss careful selection of your dog in greater detail later on.

In considering a standard versus a mini poodle, the mini can be trained to a high level of obedience too, but chances are the standard will be a kinder dog. Here again the defensiveness comes into play because of the smaller size. You might have the problems of a noisy, snappy little dog that is spoiled into obnoxious behavior by being held too much. The more you cradle your dog like a child and deny him the right to act like a dog, the greater risk you are taking of nurturing a yappy little misfit. The standard poodle is not only calmer and sweeter because of his larger size, but, for purposes of working and competition, it is easier to find a fine quality dog. They have mercifully been spared the popularity of the smaller versions, and so have been saved from such blatantly irresponsible breeding as has contributed to the slow but certain demise of many other "popular" breeds.

Dogs reflect the temperaments of their owners, and nervous, high-strung people will have nervous, high-strung dogs, even if the dog is intrinsically a calm one. Erratic behavior by the owner increases apprehension in the dog and can possibly lead to a serious behavior mistake such as biting. When people in a household are arguing, the animal will often try to find refuge in a corner, away from the crosscurrents of verbal flare. If a husband and wife, or parent and child, engage in physical aggression such as slapping or pushing, the dog will usually try to stop the stronger one, such as the husband in contest with his wife, or the mother reprimanding the child. Just as your dog has the perception to realize that he must play more gently with little people (babies and young children) and women, he instinctively comes to their defense against a male, whom he realizes is the strongest animal of the human kingdom. People who are hypertense and very erratic should try, whenever possible, to tone down this negative behavior for the mental stability of their dog. In addition, they should overcompensate by buying a dog with a supercalm temperament: a St. Bernard, Great Pyrenees, or Great Dane. A Doberman, schnauzer, or hound such as the German short haired pointer, would be quicker to bite, since these have a much shorter fuse and require less agitation to make a mistake.

Among the breeds that are anxiety chewers we find the northern dogs such as malamutes and huskies, hounds such as pointers and Irish setters, some poodles and schnauzers and many of the smaller breeds of terrier type. These high-strung dogs will find gastronomic delights abounding throughout your household possessions. Their sophisticated taste buds make them the gourmets of the dog world.

Breed Classifications

WORKING DOGS

> AKITA
> ALASKAN MALAMUTE
> BOUVIER DES FLANDRES
> BOXER
> BULL MASTIFF
> COLLIE
> DOBERMAN PINSCHER
> GERMAN SHEPHERD
> GREAT DANE
> GREAT PYRENEES
> MASTIFF

NEWFOUNDLAND
OLD ENGLISH SHEEPDOG
ROTTWEILER
ST. BERNARD
SAMOYED
SCHNAUZER (STANDARD, GIANT)
SHETLAND SHEEPDOG
SIBERIAN HUSKY
WELSH CORGI

SPORTING DOGS

CHESAPEAKE BAY RETRIEVER
COCKER SPANIEL
ENGLISH SPRINGER SPANIEL
GERMAN SHORTHAIRED POINTER
GOLDEN RETRIEVER
IRISH SETTER
IRISH WATER SPANIEL
LABRADOR RETRIEVER
VIZSLA
WEIMARANER

BREED CLASSIFICATIONS

HOUNDS

AFGHAN
BASENJI
BASSET HOUND
BEAGLE
BLOODHOUND
BORZOI
COONHOUND
DACHSHUND
GREYHOUND
IRISH WOLFHOUND
NORWEGIAN ELKHOUND
RHODESIAN RIDGEBACK
WHIPPET

TERRIERS

AIREDALE
AUSTRALIAN TERRIER
BEDLINGTON TERRIER
BULL TERRIER
CAIRN TERRIER
FOX TERRIER
SCHNAUZER (MINI)
SCOTTISH TERRIER
SEALYHAM TERRIER
WESTHIGHLAND WHITE TERRIER
WHEATEN TERRIER

NONSPORTING

BOSTON TERRIER
BULLDOG
CHOW CHOW
DALMATIAN
LHASA APSO
POODLE
SHIH TZU

TOYS

    CHIHUAHUA
    MALTESE
    PEKINGESE
    POODLE (TOY)
    PUG
    YORKSHIRE TERRIER

Breed Characteristics

AFGHANS

are usually bought by people who are going to show them in the breed ring. It is extremely difficult to show this dog in the obedience ring. The training would require many times the effort entailed for most other dogs. They are usually sold at about six months of age. Very often they are kept by the breeder until a year old, because people want to see the maturation of physical characteristics. Without superb countenance this dog would have no chance of showing, and an owner would remain with an expensive animal that requires a lot of grooming and won't want to do much more than, like Narcissus, fall in love with his own reflection in a full bathtub. Those that are qualified to show in the breed ring are usually kept in large runs or cellars, and never wear a collar because it would ruin their fur. They are often led around by their ears, as that is the only thing one can grab to get them from point A to point B. Afghans have almost no desire to please, although they are very smart. So, unless you are planning to show in the breed ring, this is not the dog for you.

AIREDALES

are bright, capable dogs. They can do police and guard work, and have been used in England and Germany for this purpose. In size, they qualify on the slight or lean edge so far as being heavy enough to stop a man in guard work. They can be chewers but, when corrected properly, will rarely continue. Housebreaking is moderately easy. They can learn obedience quickly and are good working dogs.

They might be a little snappy around rambunctious children, unless you get one with an exceptionally mild temperament. There is a tendency toward dog fighting. For most people, they would make a great all-around dog.

AKITA

is a dog with little desire to please. He is aloof, a typical northern-breed dog intensifying all the negative traits of the northern group. Sometimes the dog will not walk for you when you try to heel him, but conversely will pull you at any other time. This dog has precluded the word OBEDIENCE from his vocabulary, and would be most happy if you followed suit. He can be housebroken fairly easily, and probably won't chew too badly. This is not the dog to have if there are other dogs in the family, for the desire to fight other dogs is so strong as to overpower any obedience learned. Very difficult to train off leash and, in general, not receptive to training.

ALASKAN MALAMUTE

has the typical northern-breed traits of stubbornness, little desire to please, and affection on their own terms. They have an allergy to obedience training, and will connive with every fibre in their teddy bear bodies to try to convince you of the utter futility of the entire enterprise. They sometimes have chewing problems, but can be housebroken easily. Very good with children, and require only moderate exercise.

AUSTRALIAN TERRIER

deserves mention. There are not many around, and they have never become very popular. It is a good little dog, but not a wise choice around children. It might be a good choice for those who would like a paper-trained dog that is relatively content to remain in the house. If it is not babied excessively, it can be a very admirable companion for the sedentary household.

BASENJI

is a difficult dog to train. It is very smart but can be stubborn. They can be determined chewers but housebreak fairly easily. It is not a dog that can be left alone. Obedience can be learned but will require consistency and firm handling.

BASSET HOUNDS

are good sweet dogs. They are adaptive to a household with children, and can learn obedience and housebreaking easily. Chewing sometimes is a problem but they can respond with good results to positive correction. A good all-around dog for almost anyone.

BEAGLE

is a hunting dog with the typical propensities for distraction. It is a little harder to train and can be stubborn. They can be housebroken easily, but are also often insatiable chewers. Not the dog to leave alone all day. Usually friendly and very affectionate dogs. Great with children.

BEDLINGTON TERRIERS

are very cute-looking dogs. They can be stubborn, as they have little desire to please. Not a good choice for most people unless you happen to be a fancier of the breed. It would be less frustrating to buy a mechanical dog and paste a Bedlington head on it.

BLOODHOUNDS

are typical of hunting dogs in that there can be chewing problems and an overwhelming inclination toward distractions. They can be housebroken easily and learn obedience adequately. Fairly good dogs, but if left alone, anxiety with its subsequent chewing problems becomes all too manifest. These dogs need space to run around in. Not a dog for the studio-apartment dweller.

BORZOIS

are very shy, sedate, good dogs. They can be housebroken rapidly. However, they succumb to bullying and can be frightened easily. When trained they should be inundated with praise and limited to minimal physical corrections. They sometimes have chewing problems that can be corrected without too much difficulty.

BOSTON TERRIERS

are good all-around dogs, not quite as relaxed with children as in an adult environment. Chewing is a minimal problem. Housebreaking and obedience can be accomplished with firm consistency.

BOUVIERS DES FLANDRES

are excellent guard dogs but need a capable owner or handler. Very easy to obedience train to a very high level. Can be trained to guard level because they are fearless and respond excellently to agitation. Easy to housebreak, with no chewing problems. Because of their coats, they need constant grooming and daily brushing. This expensive and time-consuming maintenance may, for some people, outweigh their usefulness, and is the main deterrent to their use by police and army. They are wonderful with children and make an excellent family pet.

BOXERS

are good all-around dogs. They learn obedience and housebreaking easily, and in general are not problem chewers. There is a strong inclination toward dog fighting, and severe correction is necessary. Keep their associations confined to humans as much as possible. Once they experience a good dog fight, the proclivity becomes that much more intense. A good working dog that can be receptive to guard work.

BULL DOGS

are stubborn and require a lot of work and praise to learn obedience. They can be dog fighters. Housebreaking is easy and they generally do not have chewing problems. In spite of their fearsome countenances, they are sweet, affectionate, fiercely loyal dogs.

BULL MASTIFF

is in the same category as Great Danes and St. Bernards: big, calm, of sweet temperament. No chewing problems and good with children. Often a natural protector. Easy to housebreak. Very willing to please and easy to obedience train. Very loyal to family and home.

BULL TERRIERS

are very smart and responsive to obedience training. A little high strung, but easily housebroken. In general they don't have chewing problems, but can be very destructive dog fighters. Once again, they must be corrected severely for any aggressive acts towards other dogs, and should be kept away from these negative situations as much as possible. Not a good choice for children, but in an adult situation they display their most affable qualities. These dogs are fearless and tend to be excellent natural protectors.

CAIRN TERRIERS

can be snappy, nasty dogs at times, as is typical of the terrier breed. Not the greatest with children unless you happen to get a very friendly one. They have to protect themselves because of their small size, and have a very low tolerance for abuse. They can be dog fighters, chewers, and implacable pests. Easy to housebreak and very smart on obedience. A good dog for an adult that is going to be home all the time.

CHESAPEAKE BAY RETRIEVER

is a typical hunting dog that goes ape over distractions. A little stubborn. Can be obedience trained fairly easily. Needs authoritative discipline or else it can be a bully. May have chewing problems. Not the dog to be left alone all day in the house. Very good with children; a kind, sweet dog.

CHIHUAHUA

is a typical, small, defensive dog. Can be nasty if it's babied. Housebroken easily, very smart, and good on obedience. The basic attitude of the dog is that it must constantly protect itself. Not a good dog for someone with children, but ideal for an elderly person who cannot walk the dog and wants it paper trained. Very affectionate toward its master.

CHOW CHOW

is a very aggressive dog fighter. Typical northern breed, extremely stubborn, aloof, and less affectionate than most other dogs, it can easily be stimulated to bite anyone, including its owner. Capable of learning obedience if begun early. Not a good choice for anyone with children or erratic people in the household. Needs a calm environment, a steady hand, and must never be hit. Only recommended for the experienced dog person thoroughly cognizant of the shortcomings and dangers of the breed.

COCKER SPANIEL

has some chewing problems, is easily distractible, otherwise a good all-around dog. Very affectionate toward children, good on obedience, and easily housebroken.

COLLIES

have suffered an indiscriminate proliferation of the breed, with its attendant side effects, due to the surge of popularity in the '50s and '60s. They have been overbred into undesirable personality and temperament traits, and have a tendency toward blindness and hip dysplasia. Anyone who feels compelled to own a collie should choose carefully, for here love will not cover over a multitude of sins. If you can find a good one, you'll have an excellent working dog.

COONHOUNDS

are easily distracted. Can have chewing problems if left alone during the day. Need a lot of exercise. Easy to housebreak and train in basic obedience. Good with children.

DACHSHUND

is a good, sweet dog. Sometimes hard to housebreak. No chewing problems. Fairly good on obedience, as they are willing to please. Can be a little fearful of overly harsh corrections. They require lots of praise.

DALMATIANS

can chew up a whole house. They are difficult to housebreak and destructive when left alone. The temperament is aloof, with minimal desire to please. Obedience training is more difficult but can be accomplished with consistency. Don't allow them to bully you. They are great with children. A happy affectionate dog for people that are home all day.

DOBERMAN PINSCHERS

are among the best working dogs. They take to guard work naturally, can be easily agitated and obedience trained to the highest level of competency. They have a fierce desire to please and respond well to praise. The breed has become notorious for turning on their owners. This is a destructive half-truth. The other half lies in the fact that these dogs have a very low tolerance for physical abuse, and the persons tending to buy this breed are also those that excel in canine flagellation. If you play the role of the agitator, your dog needs no script to remind him he is now on the defensive. He will perform his role with eclat, and there is a good chance that you or some other member of the household could get bitten. This reaction is typical of any intelligent dog. An excellent choice for obedience competition and guard work, they can be trained to a higher level quicker than almost any other dog. Contrary to popular opinion, they are excellent in a family situation with children as long as they are not abused.

ENGLISH SPRINGER SPANIEL

is a very good dog for almost everyone. Easy to housebreak and usually has no chewing problems. They respond to positive handling, and are easy to train to a very high level. Good for people with children, whether home frequently or not. Also good for elderly people, and just about anybody.

FOX TERRIERS

can be stubborn and often have chewing problems. They are very smart but are not willing to please. Obedience training must be stringent, maintaining consistency at all times.

GERMAN SHEPHERD (ALSATIAN)

is the best all-around dog. His coat equips him to work in the most extreme temperature ranges. If you get a good German shepherd, you've got the best working dog there is. Unfortunately it is very easy to get a bad one. Due to their popularity, largely motivated by a familiarity with Rin Tin Tin, they have suffered the consequences of the "popular" dog in being bred for volume, not for quality. If you need one for guard work you will have to test it carefully, as will be discussed elsewhere in this book. If you do not scrutinize the dog's background and parents' personalities, you may have a guard dog that will panic at loud noises. Being fortunate enough to find a good one, you will have a dog capable of the highest level of obedience training, with a strong desire to please, easily housebroken, and rarely a chewing problem. Excellent with children and often a natural protector. An all-around perfect dog.

GERMAN SHORTHAIRED POINTER

is a chronic chewer, difficult to curtail. Compliant to a basic level of obedience training, gentle with children, and easy to housebreak. If you're home during the day, a very affable pet, but cannot be left alone for long periods because of extreme anxiety chewing.

GOLDEN RETRIEVER

is a big, sweet dog. Occasionally you can encounter a stubborn one or a chewer. In general, an excellent house pet with children. Possibly not too safe to leave him alone all day because of potential anxiety chewing.

GREAT DANE

is a very sweet, calm, tranquil dog. Easy to housebreak; no chewing problem past teething. A good dog for children. Can safely be left alone for hours. Low anxiety level. Will sleep all day. Not for a small or weak person: the strength and size of the dog would be overwhelming. Because these dogs mature late, they should not be obedience trained until the sixth or seventh month. If approached too early, they are fearful and can sulk and become belligerent.

GREAT PYRENEES

is calm, friendly, great with children. Usually not a bad chewer, easy to housebreak. Needs a little discipline on obedience, but basic training can be accomplished without too much of a problem. A wonderful family pet.

GREYHOUNDS

are nervous, high-strung dogs. They can be obedience trained fairly easily but need a lot of praise. They can be chewers. Sweet, affectionate dogs, they are very active and need a lot of exercise.

IRISH SETTER

is a high-strung dog that suffers from anxiety chewing. If you leave him alone, he'll become a one-dog demolition crew. For people who are home all day with children, it is a great dog. Learns obedience very easily, is very smart, and enjoys pleasing you. Needs a minimum of correction and can be housebroken easily. Very affectionate, lovable dogs.

IRISH WATER SPANIEL

can be stubborn. As a hunting dog, it yields easily to distraction. Housebreaking is not a problem. Fairly good on obedience. May have chewing problems. A sweet, friendly, intelligent dog. Excellent around children.

IRISH WOLFHOUND

can be housebroken and obedience trained with firm consistency. Because of its tremendous size, it is only suitable for those who are physically able to impose discipline on a very large, slightly aloof dog.

LABRADOR RETRIEVER

is fairly good for obedience work. A kind, sweet dog and an excellent choice for people with children. Needs extra work on distractions, as is typical of hunting breeds. Requires minimal corrections. Loves praise and will work for you willingly. Sometimes can have chewing problems if left alone for a long time.

LHASA APSOS

are affectionate dogs. Usually difficult to obedience train and house-break, they can be very stubborn, with little desire to please. Require tremendous amount of grooming and persistent attention to their coats. This dog is happiest in an adult environment. No chewing problems. Retains its cute appearance throughout adulthood.

MALTESE

are very smart, easy to obedience train, the kind of dog that always wants to stay with you. Usually will not run away from you outside. Sometimes shy, which can lead to snappy behavior with strangers. Do not baby them excessively. Can be excellent around children. Very good, sweet, all-around small dog.

MASTIFF

is classified as a gentle giant. He is very kind and sedate, and will probably sleep most of the day. Originally they were guard dogs and they take naturally to guard work. These dogs are not generally used for guard work by police or the army because of their tremendous size and the problems of transportation. With their great strength, instead of holding on to an aggressor's arm, they could easily dismember it with one bite. Because of their mammoth size, they can take physical abuse from children without responding defensively. Good all-around pets, they learn obedience fairly well on a basic level, Housebreaking is easy and they generally don't chew. This dog thrives on praise and needs minimal corrections. They should be trained at about six months of age. The mastiff is a great natural protector.

NEWFOUNDLAND

has occasional chewing problems. Easy to train and housebreak. A great dog around children. Cannot tolerate long periods of being alone.

NORWEGIAN ELKHOUND

can be a dog fighter. Good on housebreaking, a little aloof, not too amenable to obedience in general. They require firmness and consistency in handling. Can be very affectionate.

OLD ENGLISH SHEEPDOGS

are very aloof and stubborn, difficult to train. They can be chewers and wild puppies, playfully knocking over everything within reach. Very good, affectionate dogs around children, but they must never be hit for they can turn aggressive. They are quite a challenge and should only be bought by strong-willed individuals who can discipline them properly.

PEKINGESE

are popular dogs of the toy class. They are easy to train but offer some resistence to housebreaking. Usually no chewing problems. They can be left alone once they are housebroken. Good for an adult household.

POODLES

—toys, minis, standards—among the smartest of dogs. The small ones shouldn't be babied or carried excessively or they will become very possessive toward their master and defensively nippy with strangers. Very clownish and adorable, but inconsistent in regard to obedience accuracy. They learn very quickly and need almost no corrections. They'll do the hardest things just for praise. Easy to housebreak and usually don't have chewing problems. A great dog around children with the exception of the very small toy version, which is much better suited to a more mature household. The standard poodle is one of the very best choices for competition in the obedience ring.

PUGS

arc smart dogs. A little stubborn, but easy to housebreak. No chewing problems. A good dog for an elderly person who is confined to home most of the time. Poor choice for children. Can become snappy if babied.

RHODESIAN RIDGEBACK

is a very stubborn, aloof dog, with little desire to please. Much more of a challenge on obedience than most other dogs. Can be very hard to housebreak, and often has acute chewing problems. Definitely not the dog for everyone. Better suited to a rural setting.

ROTTWEILER

is a highly powerful dog that combines the physical characteristics of speed found in the Doberman and the strength of a mastiff. It is an excellent choice for guardwork and takes very well to all training. Easy to housebreak. Has a low tolerance for child-induced rough-housing, but very good in an adult situation.

SAMOYED

is a typically aloof northern-breed dog. Can respond well to obedience training if dispensed by a firm, consistent handler. May have chewing problems.

SCHNAUZER

—mini, standard, and giant—basically good dogs to obedience train. Very smart. Can be stubborn. Not a judicious choice around rambunctious children. May have chewing problems. The giant schnauzer is excellent for guard work, but the frequent grooming and clipping expense is its chief drawback for use as a guard dog by the army or police. However this should not be a serious deterrent for the private owner.

SCOTTISH TERRIER

is fairly good on obedience. Easy to housebreak. Can have chewing problems. Sometimes a little stubborn. Not the greatest dog around children; can be a little snappy. As cute when mature as it looks when only a puppy.

SEALYHAM TERRIERS

are easy to housebreak. Occasional chewing problems. Can be stubborn to obedience train. Good dog for an adult situation. Should not be nagged, babied, and coddled, or they can become snappy little rulers of the house.

SHETLAND SHEEPDOGS

are similar to collies. Possibly a better choice than a collie because they have not been inbred as much. Very good for obedience and competition, can be trained to a very high level. Easy to housebreak. Sometimes have chewing problems. Fairly good around children. May be troublesome if left alone.

SHIH-TZU

is a very stubborn dog. Small desire to please. Extremely difficult to housebreak. Very affectionate if few demands are made upon them. They love to be pampered and need a lot of praise. Apprehensive with children unless treated very gently. Can be chewers if left alone. Their coats need constant grooming to avoid matting.

SIBERIAN HUSKIES

are cute, adorable bundles of fluff when puppies, but when full grown can be difficult to control. They sometimes have severe chewing problems, and also tend to be stubborn and less than cooperative, not caring if they please you on obedience training. They need a firm hand and consistency on obedience, and training should be started early. Very sweet, affectionate dogs, good with children, these dogs should never be abused by children or adults, and should never be hit.

ST. BERNARD

is a sweet dog. Not too easy to obedience train, but easy to housebreak and great around children. A very good dog for almost anyone. Calm temperament, can be left alone all day without chewing problems.

VIZSLA

resembles a small Weimaraner. Once again, like hunting dogs, the

Vizsla is drawn to distractions, making it difficult to get his attention. Can be obedience trained to a very high level. Responds well to praise and has a good desire to please. Sometimes has bad chewing problems and becomes anxious when left alone. Needs consistency. Not a dog for everyone. Can be very sweet with children. If people are home all day, chewing problems will be minimized.

WEIMARANERS

are German hunting dogs, sometimes referred to as grey ghosts, make excellent pets. They require a great deal of exercise and, if cooped up in the house, can have severe chewing problems. They are extremely stubborn and easily distracted, and can be difficult to obedience train and housebreak. These dogs require consistent handling and firm training, and can achieve a high level of obedience skills only if the proper technique is used. If nagged, they will be unresponsive and contest your will for their entire lives. Capable of guard work, they respond well to agitation.

WELSH CORGI

is highly intelligent, easy to housebreak. Can be good with children. Usually can be left alone without chewing problems. Responds well to obedience training.

WESTHIGHLAND WHITE TERRIER

is a typical terrier, subject to slight nervousness. Easy to obedience train. Can be a little snappy around children.

WHEATEN TERRIER

has a tendency to be a dog fighter. Stubbornness, slight aggression, cannot handle too much abuse from children. Can be lovable if not babied.

WHIPPET

is shy, good on obedience, needs a great deal of praise to build up confidence. Can be a bad chewer when left alone. Easy to housebreak.

can be a very sweet dog, even around children, when not babied and coddled by an ineffective handler. Despite the small size, they have a greater tolerance to rough handling by small fry. Very good on obedience and housebreaking. No real chewing problems. A very good all-around dog.

Your Particular Situation

APARTMENT VERSUS PRIVATE DWELLING

If your apartment happens to be a walk-up, you might decide to get a small- to medium-sized dog that could be totally paper trained. If you decide on housebreaking your puppy, he will have to relieve himself about six times a day, gradually tapering to three or four outings as he attains adulthood and gains maximum control over his excretory functions. But rejoice for your pet: he will consider these outings as the high points of his day. To a dog, nothing is more fun than the sights, sounds, and smells of the great outdoors.

Living in an apartment, in close proximity to neighbors, you must have great concern not to disturb them with noise. A dog that, all day long, serenades of his unremitting loneliness, while you are out earning the Ken-L-Ration, is sure to bring down wrath against you. A dog that is at ease when left alone will minimize the risks of barking and howling. These problems would not be quite as crucial in a private home since there is more space to cushion the nerves.

For the apartment dwellers who are also working people, we would preclude most of the hunting and northern breeds and some terriers, as they are infamous for their chewing and barking. Note, the apartment alone is not the objection. It is the owners' all-day absence that creates the anxiety and its attendant problems. A good dog for the "apartment and alone" situation would be a good German shepherd, Doberman, St. Bernard, Great Dane, bull mastiff, mastiff, Great Pyrenees, poodle, Labrador or golden retriever, dachshund, or Sheltie.

German Shepherd Dog

Doberman Pinscher

Poodle

Norwegian Elkhound

Alaskan Malamute

Miniature Schnauzer

COUNTRY VERSUS CITY DOGS

Physically larger breeds could be chosen to live in the country, where room, or lack of it, is not a critical factor. They can be the hyperenergetic hunting-breed types such as the Irish setter, Chesapeake Bay retriever, German shorthaired pointer, Weimaraner, or Vizsla, who can be quietly sedate and companionable in the evening after romping in a spacious back yard all day. If this type is left at home alone for long periods, the close confinement will increase his apprehension to the point where he will make an orgiastic feast of your household contents. Given a lot of exercise and space, these dogs are in ideal environment. A word of caution for urban dwellers; games like go-and-fetch-it can be fatal on city streets. For a city dog, a smaller breed could be chosen. Many of them require no auxiliary exercise other than that they get skittering about the home. Often, neecessity dictates that they be left alone for many hours. A large dog can be a city dog if it has a calm temperament. Examples of such dogs are a good German shepherd, St. Bernard, Great Pyrenees, Great Dane, mastiff, or Labrador retriever. These dogs are all very good with children, and placid, nondestructive types when left alone.

THE CHILDLESS COUPLE

You are probably the business or professional couple who have a busy life somewhat dispersed from the nucleus of the home fires. You need a pet that is content to be left alone all day. Not one whose nerves will compel him to chomp your nearly completed masters thesis into confetti. You would also be wise to choose a dog that requires minimal exercise. Being greeted by a pet in sweat shirt and sneakers, ready for a hundred-yard dash, is quite disconcerting, especially after you've been through an exhausting day at work.

THE ELDERLY COUPLE

You have been through enough trials and tribulations in your lifetime. Now your time has come to enjoy each other, and a new member who will provide a joyful addition to your quiet household. Foremost, you don't want a dog that will require you to puppy-sit on weekends! Next, you need one that you are physically able to handle, not only for walking, but to maintain control in obedience work. Grandparents are notorious for indulging their grandchildren. Please do not allow this well-intentioned behavior to carry over to your dog. You might want to consider

THE LIBERATED LADY

buying a dog of some five or six months. Housebreaking and chewing problems are minimized at this age, the dog's temperament is pretty well formed, and the dog can often be purchased at a more reasonable price. Mixed breeds could also be considered.

THE FAMILY WITH CHILDREN

Your pet is not a wind-up toy that can be pounced upon and ridden to exhaustion, or pulled apart and reconstructed again. You cannot remedy abuse with the tightening of a few loose screws. And loose screws there will be, not in the joints, but in Fido's head. We know that *you* realize all this, but the problem is conveying it to the children, that inexhaustible group of little people who always seem to have the energy we wish we had. A big, calm dog, or even one of the hunting breeds, would be ideal for this situation. In this environment a dog must be big enough to withstand physical abuse comfortably and calm enough to accept it graciously.

THE LIBERATED LADY

requires a dog that won't be jealous of her other lovers. The dog will probably have to accept many new people coming and going. It can't be aggressive, unless you happen to be into emasculation. The size can be small or large depending upon your preferences, but a big, calm dog can serve the purpose of protection as well as companionship should you ever need it. The man who came to dinner and wants to stay all night would never be put off by a toy poodle, but will listen when a Great Dane speaks. Also, important consideration must be given to where to put your pet while you indulge your call of the wild, without his suffering rejection syndrome. Some dogs behave like eunuchs, and couldn't care less in what pleasures you indulge. If your dog acts completely bored with the festivities and shows no proclivities for group sex, he can be left in the room. If however he shows an uncanny interest in the sounds and smells of lovemaking, then give him a bone and relegate him to another room in the house. If you have a very small dog and have been making a cradle of your lap for him most of the time, it will be very difficult for the dog to accept sharing you with anyone else. Lovemaking under protest, no matter who is doing the protesting, is never very much fun.

THE LITTLE OLD LADY

usually has specific needs that differ from the elderly couple. Often, climbing up and down stairs or taking daily walks would not be practical for her. She has neither the strength nor the need for a very large dog. A small- to medium-sized breed that can be totally paper trained, and content with a relatively sedentary life, would be the ideal choice for her. It could be a six-month-old purebred dog or a mixed breed, if carefully chosen. This minimizes housebreaking and chewing problems, in addition to cost. The older the dog gets, the less desirable he is considered, only because most people want very young puppies. A dog that would chew or bark when left alone, would be fine in this situation. Terriers and small hunting breeds are a good choice, as is a toy or mini poodle. Stay away from shepherds and Dobermans or the balance of power may shift to the wrong side.

THE PERMISSIVE PARENT

is the type of person who loves his dog too much to correct it. His kind indulgence becomes a disaster area where control of his own pet is in question. This individual will often accost you in the street with a copious flow of misinformation. His gushings are calculated to intimidate you into the same state of asinine submission he enjoys with his own dog. P.P. is vehement against corporal punishment and believes problems should be approached psychologically instead of physically. This type feels that if you reason with your dog—pointing out to it that you both can achieve a most harmonious relationship if only it could find in its magnanimous heart to accede to some of your small requests—the dog would quickly rise to the occasion. Such people embrace the philosophy that all dogs really want to please their masters!

In truth, dogs are as varied in personality and motivation as people. Some will respond to your demands for the sheer pleasure of your praise. many others will obey only because of severe enforcement. Army and police attack dogs, and seeing-eye guide dogs, are reliable because they fall into this second approach to training. So we have two basic obedience attitudes; the dog that works if and when it wants to, and the one that works because it has to. Those that fall into the former group will doubtless have occasions when they will contest your demands. If you are to obtain your victory, the proper approach to obedience work will ultimately propel your pet into the latter category. The only way obedience can be real at any level of distraction is when the dog knows he responds to your command because he must. No amount of genuflecting on your part will work in anything but the most ideal of situations with no distractions. Your dog's reliability could save one or both of your lives some day. That is certainly an ultimate reward of control. You are brainwashing your dog into believing that it can never defy you and get away with it. Make absolutely certain that no laxity on your part shows him differently. Your implacable consistency will avert this possibility. If you withhold firm physical corrections, you are preventing your dog from experiencing the justifiable consequences of its negative actions. Only in its experiencing such consequences will bad habits be discontinued and good ones encouraged, by his own choice.

If you give your dog the choices between correction and praise for a given action, he will make the right decision. No dog enjoys an atmosphere of nebulous demands. Boundaries that are clearly drawn and consistent make a dog happy and secure. The natural by-product will be pride and contentment for you. A very definite impression is reached about the permissive parent who has to hide his dog in the closet whenever company arrives or condescendingly apologizes as the dog annoys his guests.

THE SHOW-OFF

We are all familiar with this type of zoological phenomenon, a cocksure rooster that crows with a terminal case of machomania and almost without exception selects a shepherd or Doberman as his unwitting victim. These two breeds have a reputation for being very smart and easy to train. They also make excellent guard dogs and command a certain inevitable awe and respect when walked down the street. Sir Show-off uses his dog to embellish his ego, and very often beats the animal into temporary submission, rationalizing that he is showing the dog who is boss! Little does S.S. realize that he is playing the role of agitator and has shortly to look forward to a confrontation with the dog's mouth. *A dog that is hit by his master will usually turn on his master.* The amount of time before it happens depends on how short a fuse your dog has. He should receive correction verbally and via a strong leash enforcement, *not* punishment manifest as physical abuse! A Doberman has much less tolerance for unjust treatment than most other dogs. Consequently this breed has been saddled with a bad reputation for turning on their masters. The best suggestion I would have for Sir Show-off, would be to get a life-sized picture of the breed of his choice and a six-foot bull whip. It is a most practical means of keeping both man and dog out of trouble.

THE SOCIETY COUPLE

are used to lots of entertaining. Your dog will be a social asset if you teach him to serve drinks and accept coats at the door. (He should understand that they must be given back!) If he is fleet of foot, a paso doble or romantic tango will charm any lady into feeling as glamorous as Ginger Rogers. "Making" on *The New York Times,* preferably the book review section, will enable Hemminghound to fit in among the most discerning of the literati. A calm, even-tempered dog that can accept chaos in the home without cracking up, and one that will not chew when left alone is what is needed in this situation. Probably a small- to medium-sized dog, such as a poodle, Scottie, or Maltese, and even some of the terrier breeds, would be a good choice.

THE SWINGING BACHELOR

The pet for Don Giovanni must be content to be left alone all day, and be prepared for lots of action at night. It is important that your pet not be so rambunctious when you arrive home as to intimidate your lady friends into a quick departure, or perhaps early submission if you happen to be a rogue. If you are a passive type and prefer being pursued, you might want to select a member of the retriever breed. He may bring you home a real prize! Stay away from the anxiety chewers, or your romantic pad will become a garbage dump overnight. There is nothing like sweeping debris by candlelight while cursing under your breath, to quell any romantic urges. Stay away from overly aggressive and protective dogs, unless you plan on remaining a bachelor for the rest of your life.

THE TRAVELER

is used to hitting the road with great frequency. Whether it be for business or esthetic pursuits, you'll need a compatible traveling companion. If he can read road maps, this is most helpful, but short of that, be thankful if he doesn't vomit all over your sample case or suit case. In all seriousness, you should select your traveling companion from among the calm, nonchewing dogs such as the shepherd, St. Bernard, or Great Pyrenees, where size permits, or even a golden retriever. Any dog should be initiated into the traveling routine fairly early, such as learning to sit, stay, and down in the car. Your dog must realize that this is a place where he also must work. We will refer to training in the car later on in this book.

THE YOUNG MARRIEDS PLANNING A FAMILY

Since you have a perceptible streak of masochism, you would be well advised to select a pet that will neutralize your proclivity for self-torture. There will be enough challenges to face when the stork drops his bundle of joy into your eager arms. The family pet should be an asset to the household. You are going to have a furry friend for eight to 16 years of your life, so it is very important not to be frivolous in your choice. Your pet must make comfortable adjustments to the addition of new members and to their growth in size and personality. The breed you choose must be good with children. If you are home all day and your family is forthcoming, you can pick from among the hunting breeds, which are nervous when left alone but wonderful with children. A small dog of terrier or toy class would not be good, for they don't tolerate children well and tend to be nippy. A dog from the working class such as the Bouvier des Flandres, boxer, Great Dane, shepherd, or St. Bernard, makes an excellent choice for a family situation, and these dogs in the working class can all be left alone without chewing problems if the wife still goes to business and the family is projected for some time in the future.

Where To Find Your Dog

Breeder, Pet Shop, Animal Shelter

When you have decided upon a suitable breed for your or your family's personal situation, the next step is looking for the breed of your choice in an appropriate place. Most people equate looking for the family pet with driving to the nearest pet shop. There are far more desirable alternatives that you should be aware of so that you can make an intelligent evaluation of your prospective pet. Don't fall into the trap of allowing your little three-year-old child to make your decisions for you. If she badgers you for a cute novelty doll that wets its pants and burps when it sits up, and you succumb, all well and good. She'll soon tire of changing diapers and listening to belching. Children are whimsical, but you must choose the family pet with logic and good judgement, not emotion and frivolity. There is a right dog for almost everyone. If you choose the cute Scottie puppy in the corner pet shop, he may be biting your children six months later because he can't tolerate the large amount of physical abuse very small children usually dish out. However he can be an excellent dog for someone else in an adult situation. Dogs should not be chosen by how cute they look as puppies. A wrong choice could mean uncute problems when the dog matures.

So the question is, where do you find your dog? If you don't just go into a pet shop and pick the cutest, most lively dog of your chosen breed, do you go into one of the big "puppy outlets" that have large numbers of purebred dogs of all breeds. Chances are, if you want a really great dog and not just an average or fair one, you will have to look elsewhere. Usually dogs in pet shops come from "puppy mills" in the South or Midwest where inbreeding runs rampant, and the end results are dogs of poor physical and mental qualities and high emotional instability.

Although these dogs are purebred dogs, with "papers," they are usually inferior in temperament. They are often in poor health, and this sickly condition pertains before, during, and after being shipped in wooden crates to the pet shop that will finally sell them. Even if the dog is in excellent health, and a perfect physical specimen, the unknown variable is once again temperament. The reason it is unknown is because you must be able to see one or both parents to be able to determine the adult temperament of your dog. A dog's temperament resembles closely, the combined personalities of both parents. You never have this option open to you in a pet shop.

One of the big plus factors of pet shop or puppy-outlet dogs is their price. The dog can be bought for less than it would cost you from a private breeder. But, in the long run, you get what you pay for. A pet shop dog may sell for $125 but can cost you $250 to have professionally trained when he is a year of age. A dog from a private breeder may initially cost you $200, but may never have the problems that require a professional trainer with his attendant additional expense.

By now we are sure you realize that we favor private breeders as the ideal places to shop for your dog. Private breeders are listed in newspapers. They advertise when they have litters of pups to sell. For some breeders this might be twice a year; for others, more or less frequently. But a breeder is never on the mass production basis that pet shops feel forced into for economic survival. Breeders mate qualitatively for temperament, as opposed to quantitatively solely for financial gain. Almost without exception, at least one parent is on the premises, and you can often get to see other members of the family a quick ride away. The more relatives you see, the more secure you can be of a judicious choice in the offspring. Local clubs of your chosen breed can also steer you to good breeders. Private breeders are listed in magazines pertaining to dogs, as are the clubs. Even though the temptation is great, you should not take the first dog that you see. Look at many. Check out the breeder's reputation through local clubs.

Some comments about mixed-breed dogs. They can be very good pets. You cannot be sure of physical size or temperament when grown because you do not know who the parents were. People will not readily flaunt a clandestine liaison. Similarly, the parent dogs prefer anonimity after the fires of passion have fizzled. Mixed breeds are cheaper than pure breeds and can be picked up at animal shelters easily and inexpensively. They can be excellent dogs for people who only want a "pet for the kids." Some owners treat an inexpensively purchased mixed-breed dog as a worthless possession, whereas an expensive purebred dog is invested with loving care and often ludicrous indulgence. It is human nature to evaluate worth with cost, but, this being a falacious and destructive assumption, should be vigorously avoided. All dogs deserve good treatment and will reflect your treatment in their behavior towards you.

Mixed breeds are not allowed in dog shows or obedience competition. The authors of this book feel that it is an unfair, snobbish attitude not to let mixed-breed dogs compete for obedience titles. Perhaps the discerning owners of many purebred dogs couldn't take the emotional outrage of having their pure dogs lose to a "mutt," a mere pariah in the dog caste. Since this could often be the case, it is safer to eliminate such a threat to their egos by simply outlawing it. If this sounds unfair to you, you're absolutely right; it does to us also. Mixed breeds show no inferiority as far as obedience training is concerned. They can often be trained to guard level if physically and emotionally capable. They can also do off-leash and advanced obedience work. Some are even easier to develop because they have no closely inbred negative traits to counteract the learning process.

When you have focused on the most suitable breed for you and the best places to look for your pup, you have eliminated about 50 percent of the risk factor normally associated with buying a dog.

41

Choosing Your Dog Through Investigation and Testing

What a dog becomes is closely and inextricably related to what his parents are; so, in testing and evaluation, you should actually be more thorough in assessing the parents' traits than those of the pups, though both are very important.

Chances are, when you go to the breeders, one or both of the parents will be there. The first thing you should do is watch the reaction of the adult dogs. How do they react to you when you walk into the house? Most probably you will see the mother. Is she afraid? Does she back away growling, or just retreat shyly? Does she try to bite you, making an all-out attack for no reason? Does she bark without restraint, or try to shower you with licks of love? Is she uncontrollable? Or, does she just look at you, come over to smell you, and then walk away, while keeping a dignified eye on you? This last behavior pattern would be the ideal reaction should you be looking for a guard dog, but it is also the most desirable behavior for any purposes. The superfriendly parent could mean a good guard dog or a wonderful dog with children. This dog could be good for many situations. The fact that she is not afraid could qualify her for guard work, and should not be discounted simply because she is overfriendly.

The dog that backs away afraid, growling and cowering, would not make a good guard dog. It may have been beaten up or abused. If a dog makes an all-out attack on you, find out his background. Has he been hit? This dog's puppies might possibly qualify for guardwork but would have to be tested further. Check the parent dogs' walking up and down stairs. Walking on a flat surface can sometimes hide a physical defect such as hip dysplasia. Take note that you are testing the parents, not the puppies, so far.

The dog that lays there on the floor, ignoring you completely, possibly asleep, you can forget about as a guard dog. This dog can probably be a good pet. Chances are he won't learn obedience too well. He doesn't know you are alive. You could slither in and abscond with the entire household contents, with scarcely more than an apathetic yawn from him.

The mother may be slightly overprotective and nervous because her puppies are there and she sees strangers in the house. Her aggression or fear is to protect her young. If you are not sure that this is the cause, she must be tested in another area all by herself, and this should be done.

In picking your puppy from the litter, once you have decided that the parents are okay, test first to make sure that the puppy can hear and see, and is physically able to walk around. Clap your hands, whistle, quietly open a refrigerator door, all of a sudden yell NO to the puppy. Was he afraid? Was the mother afraid? Moderately or excessively? Push your hands close to the puppy's face, back and forth in a wavelike motion. Is he hand shy? Why? Has he been hit? If parent and puppy are both afraid, and they haven't been hit, it may indicate that it's not a "learned" condition. See if the puppy will walk with you as you pull him gently on a leash. Call him and see if he'll come to you. In general, see if he is alert and lively. Look at the dog's teeth. Make sure they are straight, not over- or undershot. Look at the eyes and make sure they are clear, not clouded and drippy. Look at the ears. They should be clean, not waxy and odorous. Try to see the consistency of his stool, which would often indicate if he has worms.

Further testing of parents for a dog you would want for guard work would involve the owner taking the parent dog outside, quietly removing the leash, and turning and walking away. Does the dog acknowledge his owner's presence? Does he maintain proximity or stay in the general area close to the owner? This is a responsibility test for the dog. Does he sniff, run around, and make, while concurrently looking back at the owner? If the answer is yes, then you may have a dog that would qualify for the kind of responsibility that guard work entails. If the dog shows disinterest in the owner's whereabouts, and tends to take off, you had better look somewhere else.

Many breeders who are negotiating a sale with you will not let their dogs take a test. They will give you all kinds of excuses, all the way from leash laws to "the dog has no training." Don't succumb to these nebulous babblings—look somewhere else. When you want something more than just a pet, you must be prepared to be very selective.

The ultimate test of a guard dog is courage. You could have the owner walk along with the parent dog on leash, and suddenly you, or someone else, could jump out and make loud threatening noises and gestures. You can even shoot a cap pistol in the air and observe the dog's reaction. You might bang a garbage can cover against a wall as you advance threateningly, yelling at the same time. If the dog goes for you, but was friendly before, it will make an excellent guard dog. If it jumps up at you licking and wanting to be friends, you have further testing to do. At least the dog is not afraid. If she backs away and growls, she might be able to protect you, and is worth further testing. If she is afraid and cowers behind her master, she and her puppies are not suitable for guard work. You must look elsewhere.

Vicious dogs do not make good guard dogs. They are overly aggressive and beyond the owner's control. Usually they must be put away in a cellar or some other place of confinement when people come to the door, because they cannot be trusted not to bite. A dog can't offer you any worthwhile protection unless he can be with you in situations of potential danger. A good guard dog is a very controllable dog that knows when to react through your command, or on his own, but only to unfriendly, threatening people.

The degree of importance attached to the testing of your dog would be determined by the requirements you set for him. Should you want a "working" or guard dog, testing is extremely important for determining behavior traits. If your only requirement is a pet for the family, then less critical evaluation would be required on temperament. However you would want to be painstakingly meticulous in testing the dog's health and physical characteristics. Minutes spent on testing can save months of frustrating problems later on. This is time very well spent.

Puppy Problems

BARKING—

is a natural thing in all dogs. The primal relationship that wild dogs had with man was to guard and protect a designated area by lying around the perimeter as a territorialist, barking at the approach of strange animals or unfamiliar people. In return for this service they would be thrown left-over scraps of food. This was the first kind of domestication or friendly relationship between man and dog, and it has developed into the closest, most unusual relationship between man and any animal on earth. When a dog barks at a noise and warns you, he is reacting to a primary, natural instinct. That is why dogs take to it so readily, should you wish to train them to bark on command. No other animal, including the smartest monkey in the world, will show the devotion that some dogs will. Extraordinarily devoted dogs have had to be killed once they witnessed the untimely demise of their owners. The dedication is so intense that nothing and no one can replace the loss they have experienced. Some guard dogs will sit upon their masters' graves, refusing to eat, until they die.

The approach needed to stop your dog from unwanted or excessive barking is simple basic consistency. He must never be praised for barking when you are home, then expected to remain mute when you leave. If you decide that you don't want barking, it must be NO all the time. Whenever he barks, he gets corrected. When he stops he gets praised.

The dog that barks when you are not home is reacting to fear. He doesn't know if you are coming back. He may be chewing, howling, making on your floors, with all this troublesome behavior stemming from anxiety. Usually the biggest offenders are in the hunting and terrier breeds. Since he does these things when you are not home, leash corrections cannot be utilized. If you use leash corrections when your dog barks in front of you, some of the correction may carry over to when you are not home. Often, however, this is not the case, so other methods of correction are needed. By understanding why your dog barks, you can begin to approach the problem with good judgment instead of irrational anger.

A possible solution would be very short departures of three to five minutes, with quick returns, barging in and correcting him when he barks, and praising as he stops. He can have the leash on since you are only leaving him for a few minutes. Show your dog that you can catch him in the act and correct him. You are also building up his confidence that you will return.

The next step would involve more drastic measures. If you live in an apartment and are threatened with eviction unless you can keep the dog quiet, go to greater correction. Some owners think that giving the dog away is easier than moving. We find that most dogs that are given up to new owners or to animal shelters have a less than ideal existence and often do not live very long. Dogs die from loneliness or despair, and we are all also aware that in overpopulated dogdom, if your pet can't be placed in a short space of time, he will often be destroyed. Now your dog's life is in danger, so we can justify more drastic measures.

The throw chain will be used when you are around the dog or can re-enter the house quickly without warning. The throw chain is a medium-sized choke collar with a couple of small key rings through the center to keep it compact. When you are home you can correct your dog by

"I JUST DON'T UNDERSTAND WHY HERMAN IS THE ONLY DOG ON THE BLOCK WHO CRIES AND BARKS ALL DAY LONG WHILE WE'RE AT WORK!"

throwing the chain sharply at his rear end as he is barking, and then praising him when he stops. The throw chain is only used on the rear portion of the dog and should be thrown sharply *when he is not looking at you*. It is never thrown at the front of the dog or at any part of the dog when he is looking at you. A hit in the eyes with a throw chain can cause permanent, irreparable damage. When used correctly, the throw chain can produce results that nothing else can equal. The target area will be from the middle of the dog's back to the beginning of his tail, and midway along the sides back to his rear end. Since quite accurate hits are necessary with the chain, you must be relatively close to the dog to insure hitting one of the target areas. This means never standing more than approximately ten feet from the dog when throwing. It is very important not to miss, so you must determine how closely you need to stand to accomplish this. If you never indicate to your dog that you do miss, he will never know that you can. It is important that you never miss.

The throw chain can be utilized in your presumed absence if the dog has been properly conditioned to its effectiveness when you are home in correcting barking, jumping on beds, etc. If he has been severely corrected with the chain, in front of you, he will learn to respect just the sound of it when you are out of sight.

One way to correct him for barking when you are not home is to simulate a situation where you are leaving, and leave a window slightly open in the room where the dog remains. This specific measure is only for owners of private homes and for ground-floor dwellers. Watch at the window that has been left ajar. When the dog proceeds to bark, throw the chain quickly through the window, aiming for the general vicinity of the dog. You are not aiming for the dog only throwing so that he hears it. The residual effects of the preliminary corrections will work for you now. If your dog continues to bark, have another chain ready, and throw it, being most careful that he does not see you. Leave several windows open for your operations so that you may move from one point to another, gaining the most advantageous position. The dog must think that a lightning bolt struck from the heavens. If he finds out that you are pulling the strings, the effectiveness will be considerably diminished.

Another method of out of sight correction would be to suspend one or more throw chains individually, on pieces of string or strong thread, over doorways or windows or both. Leave the premises, to return quietly and, at the sound of barking, cut the string. The suspended throw chain will drop to the floor and deter your dog from further protestation. Cut the threads one by one, as many times as needed till the barking stops. If you are a ground-floor dweller, you can suspend chains over windows and doors. If you live in an apartment, you may be restricted only to entry doorways.

In order to test the efficacy of the throw chain technique, you may want to use a tape recorder. Place it on "record," so that you can tell when, how often, how consistently, and for what purposes your dog is barking. If he is barking in protest for being left alone, he will usually cease after the first five or ten minutes. This is the most critical period of adjustment. Perhaps the tape recorder will reveal that your dog has heard someone aproaching the door. That bark has the utility of warning, and for most people should not be discouraged. However if the barking is troublesome to neighbors, unremitting and unjustified, you may want to use the tape recorder as a training aid. Place the machine on "record," and utter the word NO loudly, at intervals of four to five minutes, for a total period of 15 to 20 minutes. Then test this on your dog by placing the recorder on "play" and pretending to leave the house. Stay near enough that you may be able to test the effectiveness of the technique. The first loud NO should be timed to blast off shortly after you have left. If the barking subsides with each successive NO, then you have successfully intimidated your dog into believing you can correct even when you are not visible to him.

The key to effectiveness in uttering the word NO on the recorder lies in the prerequisite obedience work on leash, where the dog associates the word NO with a strong physical correction. This association is what will carry over to elicit the desirable response.

In order to be fair with the dog in meting out the appropriate number of NO corrections, try a dry run of about a week. Leave the house an hour or so before you really have to, and listen for the dog's response. Continue to use the corrections until they are completely effective. Then when you really must leave, place the tape on "record" for the day so that you can discover what really transpired. In this way you will not be doling out unjust punishment to your pet.

If your dog is confined in a small area for housebreaking or other purposes, enlarging the area can sometimes serve to reduce or eliminate the barking. Dogs get up-tight in small spaces. If it is not practical to enlarge the area of freedom, then a gate at the doorway will be a compromise far preferable to a closed door. This creates some illusion of space and freedom, as the dog can look through the gates and not feel isolated.

Sometimes companionship can be the answer for your dog. If you bring a cat into the household, the favorable distraction of this newfound playmate can serve to deflect his obsession with barking. Yummy-tasting marrow bones can sublimate the desire to bark, as can soothing music on the radio that also serves to drown out street noises.

If you are using any of these methods to correct your dog's barking habit, you must never praise him, or ignore some barking that you may decide is desirable. He must always be corrected for barking. The effectiveness of any of these measures depends upon complete consistency on your part. Your dog's mental balance relies on this too. There is no way he could rationalize your schismatic behavior. He would know that you are praising and punishing him alternately for the same thing. That is enough to make any dog a full-fledged neurotic.

Should all else fail, a much more drastic measure is necessary: an electrical shocking device inside a thick, heavy leather collar. This appliance can be purchased at large pet-supply outlets, or may be ordered through magazines and publications dealing with dogs and specialty supplies. The price range for this device is $20 to $30. The collar will produce maximum results for you very quickly. In a matter of minutes your dog will stop barking because his barking activates the collar and he receives a very unpleasant shock. A dog will bark two or three times with this collar on, then quickly realize that his barking is what causes the shock, thereby inducing him to stop promptly. Put this device on your dog only for 15 to 20 minutes at a time, and pretend to leave. Never leave it on for longer periods or go away and leave him with the collar on for the day. After he learns not to bark with the collar on for short periods, you can then put a dummy collar on him and leave for the day. The dog believes this to be the real thing, so you will then have the desired results without the dangers. You can take the device out of the collar, or deactivate it by removing the battery. Only in extreme cases of problem barking should this method be used. If you will otherwise have to give away your dog should he not cease barking, then this method is justified. The danger of the collar lies in the fact that it is activated by noise. This means that it could be activated by a radio, electric garage opener, television, or any type of electronic gadget. If the dog was shocked at times for no justifiable reason, the results could be disastrous. NEVER LEAVE YOUR DOG ALONE WITH THE COLLAR ON, AND NEVER LEAVE IT ON FOR MORE THAN 20 MINUTES AT A TIME, NO MATTER WHAT THE MANUFAC-TURER SUGGESTS. THIS METHOD IS TO BE USED ONLY IN EXTREME CASES OF BARKING.

BITING—

can be divided into two types. One is puppy mouthing, a reaction to teething pain. This same pain also contributes to puppy chewing problems. The other type of biting progresses in predictable stages, beginning with aggressive growling, curling lips, light nipping, and advancing into all-out attack. The first problem is minimal and generally will be outgrown by about six months.

If you are not sure which type of biting problem you have, if your dog is a year old and still biting, don't wait around for him to outgrow it. The puppy biting can be curtailed considerably by the application of a leash correction when your dog is mouthing, using a jerk on the leash and yelling a firm NO; then by contrast, praising him immediately when he stops. There is no malice involved in puppy mouthing. The puppy will actually be rubbing his gums and teeth on you to obtain relief from intense teething pain. If you can divert him to his chew toys, making them very desirable with the scent of raw bacon rubbed on them, contrasted with the use of *alum* applied to things that he must not chew, such as his leash, your shoes, or the furniture, the contrast will enable him to make the right choice. Alum is a white powder that can be purchased in drug stores. Mix with water to a paste consistency and apply it to all surfaces except velvet. If your dog eats alum, don't let him have any water. Water serves to reduce the bitter taste in the dog's mouth, sending him right back for a repeat performance. A bowl of ice cubes or a frozen wash cloth, will provide favorable relief from teething pain. Leather rawhide chew toys are very good, but rubber toys are useless for relieving this pain.

The mature dog that develops into an aggressive biter is in terrible danger. He will eventually bite someone who has no tolerance or sympathy, who could press charges, and your dog might have to be given up to the pound to be destroyed. Nobody wants a dog that bites him, and giving it away to another person only compounds the problem because it will just be a matter of time until he bites the new owner too.

The biting dog must be dealt with quickly and forcefully. If the problem is still in the early stages, he can be physically corrected with a jerk on the leash, and a very decisive NO as used in the obedience training. When he stops, praise him. This correction must be much more severe than in implementing a sit correction, because the offense is much graver. A dog should never be allowed to bite and get away with it. If he bites, or shows overt aggression, he should be put right back into the same situation or a similar one and induced to try it again. The reacting

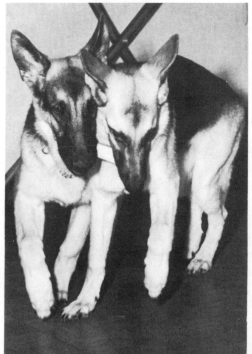

HAVING A PLAYMATE CAN
SOMETIMES QUELL THE
BARKING URGE

RAWHIDE OR NATURAL BONE
CAN PROVIDE A "HEAVENLY"
DISTRACTION FOR A
BARKING DOG

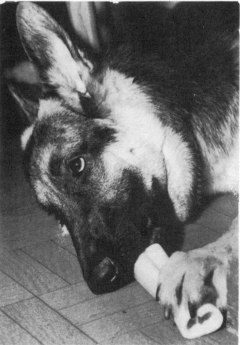

physical correction should be as harsh as you can muster. Never correct five or ten minutes after your dog has bitten someone. He must be disciplined as he attempts to bite. This is very important.

There are many reasons why a dog will bite. Often it has been hit or beaten in an attempt to correct other problems, such as making in the house or chewing. This mistreatment often festers till the dog reaches adulthood, at which time frustration perverts itself into a full-blown biting problem. Dogs should never be beaten. A dog that is hit will bite. They should be corrected with the same leash corrections that you would use for obedience training. Basic obedience training, which incorporates the correction methods for biting problems as well, can effectively correct the dog who is beginning to get aggressive. If a dog has been getting away with biting for some time, and cannot be quelled by strong physical corrections, then the problem should be turned over to a professional trainer. Possibly the best way to do this would be to have a professional trainer come into the home and eliminate this problem for you there through his skill and guidance. If done in the home the dog cannot be abused, but if taken away to a kennel you have no control over the methods of correction used and the dog may be mistreated.

Dogs that are hit usually bite the one who has hit them. Sometimes they will victimize a weaker member of their family, a stranger, or a combination of all. A dog must learn through obedience training that what may have been tolerable before is no longer acceptable. Guard dogs are trained by hitting and teasing, thereby building up their aggression in a special way. So you would never want to take the role of the agitator and have your own dog build anger and annoyance to the point where he will turn on you. A dog that is hit may subdue the blossoming aggression he feels toward the agitator, but redirect his anger at a weaker figure, as, perhaps, the wife or a small child.

A warning bark is very different from an all-out attack. The misguided people who condone their dog's unprovoked biting of strangers in the street, or visitors who are properly admitted to the house, are inviting negative consistency elsewhere. If it is okay to bite these people sometimes, eventually it will be okay to bite anyone anytime. You must never indulge your dog's unjustified aggression toward others. Biting should be prevented whenever possible, and stopped absolutely, once begun. The price of indulgence can be your dog's life, and the physical safety of your family and others.

CHEWING—

There are two kinds of chewing. One is caused by teething pain in a puppy, and usually lasts until the dog is about six months of age. This is normal, and should be expected. The other kind is nervous—anxiety—chewing that continues past the teething stage and exasperates many owners into wanting to part company with their pets. Nervous chewing can persist to any age and is much harder to stop. Usually anxiety chewing is not demonstrated in front of you, whereas puppy chewing is often done *on* you as well as in front of you, being a full-time vocation for your pup. The puppy who is teething, will mouth your hands, chew your shoes, the leash, and anything else he can reach. This can be corrected by grabbing the leash and yelling NO, as you jerk on the leash. When he stops, praise him—GOOD BOY—allowing him to choose between the correction and the praise. If you are consistent, he will make the right choice. Always have a line dragging when you can watch your dog, and correct consistently in this manner. Don't forget the praise when he stops, or you will be eliminating the contrast between correction and praise that will make him want to do the right thing. Don't yell NO and then the dog's name, for he will associate his name with a negative thing. If you want him to stop jumping up and mouthing you, don't shout DOWN. That command means something else very specific. NO is used for any negative behavior. Make your delivery more forceful and vociferous than for any of the other commands you will be teaching your dog, such as HEEL, SIT, and DOWN. Consistency being the byword, do not chastise your pet for mouthing some people, while others are allowed or even encouraged to play tug-o-war with arms and leashes and fingers flying. Never allow your dog to use his leash as a plaything or chew toy. The above physical corrections are to be used when your dog chews in front of you.

All dogs feel a certain anxiety when you leave them alone, worrying if you will return. The ones that feel this apprehension most acutely are the high-strung anxiety chewers. Their problem is much more severe, more difficult to stop. Destruction appears to be spitework but, in fact, is extreme anxiety over your anticipated return. If you return home and find a flagrant display of ruin, do not react like a bull in a china shop. Your dog will only become more distraught and, in addition, will fear your return as well as your departure. Very few dogs are capable of true spitework. The howl that you hear from your dog upon leaving the house is an indication of pure misery. He doesn't know if you are going to come back. The same dog that is an anxiety chewer, can also be an anxiety barker,

53

howler, or piddler when you are not home.

So, when you can't be with your dog, he very probably still requires correction for chewing. The method advised is to introduce something that will cause a bad taste in his mouth when you are not around to correct him. That something is alum, and its use was described under BITING. Alum has a very bitter taste and will make your dog quite thirsty. See that he doesn't get near any water, or he will be able to relieve the bitter taste in his mouth and come back for more. Withhold water for one hour if you see that your dog has eaten alum.

Some dogs are not deterred by the taste of alum. If you find yours falls into this category, use Chinese mustard, tabasco sauce, or a preparation sold in grooming and pet shops or at your vet's called Bitter Apple. One or another of these preparations is bound to work on most any dog. Your dog will discover that some things taste horrible and others, like his chew toys, taste very good. To provide a further inducement in the right direction, rub a piece of raw bacon on his chew toys before you leave home, making those objects irresistible. You can't stop an anxiety chewer, so you have to direct his chewing towards acceptable objects.

In more extreme cases of chewing, accompanied by barking and howling where you are faced with an eviction notice or the need to get rid of your dog, we would justify the throw can as a possible solution. If you are in a ground-floor apartment you could pretend to leave your house, and perhaps get someone else to pull away in your car. Then return to a slightly opened window where you know the dog is confined, and throw an empty soda can with some pennies in it near the dog. The greatest amount of destruction is done within the first 15 minutes after you have left. Your dog will begin to realize that bad things can happen even when you are not home. Line up ten cans, if you have to, and throw them when needed. The dog will be learning that you can correct him even when you are not home. Another method is to prerecord an hour-long tape, with your voice yelling NO every five to ten minutes. The hour-length tape is usually long enough to make your presence felt at prime destructive time. As in the corrections for barking, experiment with this method before you really have to leave, so your dog will not receive unjust punishment. Set aside a half-hour to an hour before leaving the house to watch your dog carefully from a window. Burst in on him as soon as he starts to chew, yelling NO. This will condition him for the sound of your voice on tape when you really are gone. After a half-hour to an hour of this preconditioning, your dog will be convinced that you can barge in on him at any time. Your neighbors will also be convinced that you are a Peeping Tom, and they might even call the police. But anything is justified to salvage your dog, even if you do become known as the town pervert.

For more drastic cases, where none of the above solutions work, a more extreme measure is needed. This would take the form of mousetraps set with paper wrapped around them, as shown in the accompanying diagram. The mousetraps set up in this way could be taped to sides or legs of tables and chairs or placed on tops of couches, tables, and beds. They can even be placed on or hidden in garbage bags or cans. The mousetraps go off when touched, hitting the paper and making a loud noise that discourages the dog from further pursuit of the forbidden object. The dog is not hit or hurt by the mousetrap itself. This is one more measure that can be effective when you are not home. *Never set traps without first wrapping paper around them as indicated in the diagram.*

TOP VIEW
PAPER IS WRAPPED
AROUND LOADED
MOUSETRAP.

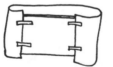

BOTTOM VIEW
PAPER ENDS MAY BE
TAPED TO BOTTOM OF
TRAP, AS SHOWN.

SIDE VIEW.

This method should provide correction, not torture, for your dog. Occasionally you will find a dog so big and tough that he will just snap the trap and brush it aside, or even chew it to pieces.

If your dog chews in front of you, use the leash correction while yelling NO. When he stops praise him immediately, saying GOOD BOY. Any chewing that persists, despite all of the methods suggested, requires the attention of a professional trainer.

FEEDING—

We recommend canned food with meal or cereal. Dry, dehydrated dog food in cereal or burger form makes your pup very thirsty and more difficult to housebreak or paper train. The consumption of large quantities of water will make him urinate more often.

An average dog that would eat a can of dog food (beef flavor preferably, because they don't need variety) would require about two to three cups of meal with it. Specific diets will be described in detail in the housebreaking chapter, as far as what and when to feed, and the quantity for different ages and weights of dogs.

A word about table scraps. Feed them to your dog if you must, but only with the regular meals and *only at the times designated on the feeding schedule.* There is always the risk that your dog can become a picky eater once he is spoiled on people food. If he doesn't know anything better exists, he will be very content eating his dog food,. Should your dog start to hold out for the more tasty food he thinks is coming, eliminate table scraps from his diet completely. We recommend dispensing with table scraps entirely. Additionally, all the different colors and shapes in

SOME PEOPLE ALLOW THEIR DOG'S
FEEDING TO GET OUT OF HAND

dog biscuits are geared to pleasing people. Do you really believe he cares whether he eats a toy train or a fire engine? The dog doesn't know the difference and can only see in black, white, and tones of grey. So, if you must indulge, understand whom you are indulging.

Puppies under three months of age can have four meals a day. At three to six months of age they can have three meals a day. At six months on into adulthood, they should taper down to two meals a day and continue eating twice daily for the remainder of their adult lives. Most people think one meal a day is enough for a grown dog, but this is not true any more than it is so with humans. It is easier on the dog's digestive system if the feeding cycle is broken into two parts. The morning meal can be light, but it will be enough to round out the dog's digestive processes.

GROOMING—

A dog such as the German shepherd or Doberman pinscher will not need professional grooming, but a dog like the poodle or schnauzer definitely will. Such things should be taken into consideration before purchasing your puppy. Will you be able to afford the monthly cash outlay that professional grooming requires? A low-maintenance dog needs little more than daily brushing, which stimulates the oil glands of the skin, rids the dog of loose hairs that are shedding, prevents matting, and loosens surface dirt and dandruff. Every dog should be brushed at least every other day. Where your dog's coat is found to be dry, your vet may recommend one or two drops of mineral oil once or twice a week with his food. This should not be taken more frequently or it will cause diarrhea and seriously disturb the housebreaking routine. If your dog nervously chews on himself, this can be stopped by applying a coat conditioner directly to the area. It will have a bitter taste, repelling the dog from doing further damage to himself.

You should clean and inspect a dog's ears once to three times weekly. A cotton ball dipped in mineral oil or baby oil should gently swab the inside of his ears. Dogs like a German shepherd that have open erect ears are rarely prone to ear infections. The dry surface discourages potential bacteria from nesting. Dogs with ears that flop over, such as poodles and most of the hunting breeds, have interior ear surfaces that tend to remain moist. This is a favorable breeding ground for bacteria and infection. The ears of these dogs must be scrutinized closely and cleaned regularly two or three times weekly. If you smell a foul odor emanating from your dog's ears or notice large deposits of waxy crusts, home remedies are no longer practical. This is now a job for your vet. Preventive maintenance will minimize serious infections from developing, with ensuing complications and expense. Having the vet clean your dog's ears before they become infected is relatively inexpensive. It is prudent for your purse as well as your pet to indulge in this extra bit of care. Never use cotton swabs on a stick to clean the dog's ears. If the dog moves suddenly, they can penetrate the ear canal, rupturing his ear drum.

An occasional nail clipping will suffice if your dog goes for daily walks, because the abrasiveness of a pavement acts as a natural nail file. Try to leave the nail cutting for your vet or groomer because there is always a danger of cutting into the quick, especially on dark-nailed dogs, and causing unnecessary bleeding. For those who are going to clip their dog's nails, more frequent clipping is preferable to lopping off a great quantity of nail at one time.

Dogs don't needs baths as frequently as people think they do. Three to four times a year is enough. A dog should be kept in a warm, dry place after a bath; he should not be allowed out until thoroughly dry. A good way to insure this would be to bathe the dog after his final walk at night. If he is bathed in the bathtub, you can use a wet dog shampoo that your vet would recommend and possibly sell to you. The most desirable products for the bath will not be found on supermarket shelves. You may not even find them in your local pet shop. It is well worth any extra expense to get a quality product from your vet. Human soaps and shampoos should not be used because they tend to be alkaline, causing drying, itching, flaking, and other general discomforts. The dog could be dried off with towels or a hair dryer. He should have all night to dry off and cool off, so that he can't go outdoors and possibly catch pneumonia. This is a very real danger, so dogs should be kept inside for at least four hours after their baths.

Minimal care is necessary for your dog's teeth. Rawhide and marrow bones provide enough abrasion to get rid of excess tartar and the accompanying bad breath in your dog's mouth. Steak and chicken bones are extremely dangerous for your dog. They can splinter when chewed, and can be fatal. Dogs do not generally get cavities, but can incur certain gum disorders. An adult dog's teeth can be cleaned occasionally by your vet, but only if he recommends it for excess tartar in your dog's mouth.

Some breeds such as St. Bernards, Great Danes, pugs, and Pekingese are particularly prone to eye problems and eye infections. Dogs whose long hair hangs over the eyes, such as terriers, poodles, and Old

English sheepdogs, must be groomed properly and regularly to prevent dirt from entering the eyes. Any continued irritation, dripping, or scratching should be checked out by your vet.

All dogs should be checked every other day along the pads of their feet, for cuts, burrs, and thorns. The entire body should be carefully investigated by hand for burrs and ticks with equal frequency.

A side benefit of all the care in grooming, handling, and checking for burrs, scratches, etc., is that your dog will be conditioned to being handled by you and other responsible members of your household. No area on a dog should be out of bounds to his master's touch, but the liberty, likewise, should not be abused. The peripheral advantages are in the area of obedience. Get your dog used to your touch gradually by initiating him at a very early age. He is less apt to be fearful of the consequences of touching if he has been initiated slowly and wisely. Many dogs will come to enjoy brushing, along with a moderate degree of handling. Your pet will also be more tolerant of children's probing little hands.

JUMPING—

Jumping on people is an obedience problem, a social offense that will be corrected through the dog learning basic obedience. With obedience training he will be utilizing his mind more fully in exercising the discretion of choice, and he will also be learning the value of a NO correction and his role in responding to it. There is no justifiable reason for your dog to use people as tackling dummies. He would be thrilled at your complicity in his gymnastic feats. But if you succumb, your friends will opt for calling you on the phone or writing letters in lieu of facing the bouncing dog.

Your dog should be corrected as he jumps up, by jerking on the leash and yelling NO forcefully. Praising him, once he has stopped, creates an all-important contrast. This method is a basic, effective way to stop a dog from jumping. Another method of correction would be a knee lift into the chest, but children and elderly people would find it most difficult to implement this form of correction with the proper force and timing. The correction could be misconstrued as a game by your dog, if not done correctly. Also, strangers entering the house will not be able to, and should not be expected to give this correction. The arrogant familiarity on the part of a visitor, in attempting this correction, could cost him his kneecap or worse.

ALTHOUGH YOU MAY ENJOY AN OVERZEALOUS GREETING FROM YOUR PET, YOUR GUESTS WILL NOT!

Therefore leash corrections work best on this problem, and it is your responsibility to correct until you win out. If your dog bobs back for more, he is telling you that he needs harder corrections. Remember, you should be applying a leash jerk, not becoming one.

He should be corrected every time he jumps on you or someone else, and praised when he stops. Do not use the command DOWN when you want him to stop jumping up. DOWN will mean something very different and specific to him when he learns to lie down on verbal command and hand signal. Use only the word NO loudly, and with a leash correction, for everything negative that you want him to stop. Going into a wild oration or chastising your dog with a flailing index finger in his face will only make him more confused and, along with it, perhaps fearful or aggressive.

Never tell your dog to do anything that you cannot back up with a correction if he disobeys you. Don't let him think that he can declare a holiday from obedience when he so chooses. Let him drag three or four feet of clothesline on a choke chain while you are home with him in the house. Always take the clothesline off when your dog is being left alone. The only thing that can remain on, if you so choose, is a properly fitting collar.

The corrections for jumping will get better results if used in conjunction with obedience training. The more you give a dog to do, the busier he will be thinking of living up to these demands, and the less likely he is to be blatantly obnoxious.

His name should never be used in conjunction with the word NO: he will begin to associate his name and himself with the negative thing that he is being corrected for.

Dogs should never be tied up and left alone. In absolute emergency, if you must tie him up, then use a strap collar. Never leave him tied to a choke chain. The strap collar will not tighten around his neck and choke him. The choke collar can sometimes contort and knot, making it impossible to release. *You could kill your dog by being careless in this way.*

MEDICAL CARE—

One of the puppy problems you will have to face is resisting the temptation to walk your puppy in the street until after he gets certain required shots. This will defer total housebreaking for a short time. Your pup should not be permitted to walk, sniff, and make where other dogs have eliminated. Contact with other dogs' excretory matter can make him fatally sick. You will have to paper train your pup for an interim period that lasts about a month. Puppies are usually deemed safe for the street at three months of age. By this time they will most likely have had all the necessary shots to protect them from disease. Follow the advice of your own vet on these matters. If you have a fenced-in back yard that other dogs can't get into, then your pup can be taken outside without all the other accompanying risks.

A frequent problem with puppies is worms. This can be diagnosed positively by a stool sample; the dog does not have to go to the vet. Simply put the most recent stool sample in a container and bring it to your vet. If it is diagnosed as positive, then your dog should be brought in for treatment. The treatment for worms is very important. The second follow-through treatment is the all-important thing in worming your dog. The larvae are born two or three weeks after the initial worming. The first worming may kill all the adults. The dog appears to be better. His bowels are hard again but your troubles are not over yet. Three weeks later he is reinfested as the larvae are born. If your vet has not suggested a follow-up visit and worming two to three weeks after the first, suggest it to him and *make certain it is done.*

If a dog has worms, he is going to have a constant churning in his stomach. He is not going to be able to be housebroken. His defecation will be soft and ongoing, causing discomfort, irritability, fatigue, and listlessness. This will affect obedience training as well as the dog's entire attitude.

Get rid of the worms as quickly as possible. All worms cannot be seen in the stool; some can only be detected under a microscope. If your dog defecates alternately soft and hard, making more frequently than three times a day, he is a sick dog. Do not go to a store and buy medication attempting to worm the dog yourself. Go to the vet and get the job done right. The medication may consist of a shot or pills, depending upon the kind of worms. Almost all puppies have worms that, if medicated promptly, can be eliminated completely in less than a month. Once your pup is free of worms, housebreaking or paper training can be accomplished successfully.

There is one kind of worm that is always fatal to your dog: the heartworm. While there is no cure, there is a simple way of protecting your dog. Your vet will test the dog for heartworm by taking a blood sample. If the dog is free of it, the vet will prescribe tablets to be taken daily according to your dog's weight. This will offer thorough protection if given as directed. Dogs get heartworm from mosquitos, who are carriers of the infection. The mosquitos bite dogs, infusing them with the disease. If your dog takes the pills all during the mosquito season, April to November, he will be safe.

As far as giving your dog vitamins, follow your vet's recommendations. Milk can be given once a week, but not every day. Milk and cheese, when fed too frequently, cause diarrhea and consequent housebreaking problems. This book contains a diet chart in the chapter on housebreaking. Should your vet override this, it would be for a specific need of your dog and his advice should be followed.

For eye, ear, teeth, and nail care, see GROOMING. If you notice any unusual developments, consult your vet.

PAPER TRAINING—

The best time to bring your puppy home is when he is approximately eight to 12 weeks old. He should be brought to the vet immediately, and checked out thoroughly. Your agreement with whomever you purchased the dog from should be contingent upon perfect health, or immediate refund or exchange. This agreement should be in writing. A handshake is a nice friendly gesture, but it doesn't hold much water when a battle of rights ensues.

As a general rule, keep your puppy away from other dogs and places where other dogs have urinated and defecated. He can pick up diseases from these sources very quickly because he has not yet been vaccinated against primary sources of infection. The ideal place to initiate your dog's excretory functions would be an enclosed back yard that no other dogs can get to.

Since young pups should not be allowed on the street until they have certain injections, you will have to paper train for an initial period, until the time you can convert to housebreaking. This period could last from one to four weeks. Choose the area in which you would like him to make. Preferably, this should be a small room. Put papers down, covering the entire floor surface. Right after the dog eats, place him on papers. Clean up the first elimination, reserving one newspaper to retain the scent. This will now be placed on top of a fresh pile of newspapers. A dog's sense of smell is seven times more powerful than that of a human, so he will be able to locate his spot from that one newspaper, even though the smell eludes you. Repeat this process of conserving one newspaper until your dog zeros in on one particular area where he has gone again and again. Never use a suppository on your dog for purposes of housebreaking or paper training.

The papered area is gradually reduced in size, until it is only as big as necessary for your dog. This may be as small as one foot square for a small toy dog.

Schedule for eight-week to six-month-old puppy. Three or four meals a day, food left down for ten minutes only. Water, as much as he will drink, but only at times designated on schedule.

> 6:50 First thing in the morning, put dog on papers.
> 7:00 Food, water
> 7:10 Put dog on papers
> 10:30 Food, water
> 10:40 Put dog on papers
> 1:00 Food, water (dogs under three months get
>   fourth meal at this time)
> 1:10 Put dog on papers
> 4:00 Food, water
> 4:10 Put dog on papers
> 7:00 Water, put dog on papers
> 9:00 Water, put dog on papers
> 11:30 Put dog on papers (NO WATER)

If you decide to continue paper training for the life of the dog, then follow the schedule for six-months-and-older dogs. If not, as soon as your puppy can go outside, switch to housebreaking routine and schedule.

Schedule for six-months-and-older dogs. Two meals a day. (Preferable to gulping all at one time.) Give all the water your dog will drink, but only at times indicated.

> 6:50 First thing in the morning, put dog on papers.
> 7:00 Food, water
> 7:10 Put dog on papers
> 11:00 Water, and put dog on papers
> 3:30 Food, water
> 3:40 Put dog on papers
> 7:00 Water, and put dog on papers
> 11:30 Put dog on papers (NO WATER)

Typical puppy schedule for people that both work.

> 6:50 First thing in the morning, put dog on papers.
> 7:00 Food, water
> 7:10 Put dog on papers·
> 8:30 Water, and put dog on papers

> Confine dog in a large safe area, with papers available.

> 5:30 Food, water
> 5:40 Put dog on papers
> 9:00 Water, and put dog on papers
> 11:30 Put dog on papers (NO WATER)

In cases where three meals are necessary, as with dogs under five months old, an 8:00 PM feeding and 8:10 placement on papers can be added to the above schedule.

If your dog makes a mistake in another area of the house, use a specially designed deodorizer such as liquid Nilodor, which is a concentrate. Use 15 drops to three cups of water and keep this solution in a jar for repeated use. No commercial cleaner such as bleach, ammonia, pine disinfectants, or novelty sprays will work. The dog's nose knows the difference, and he will find his spot again and again, much to your chagrin.

Irish Setter

Boxer

Vizsla

Shih–Tzu

Great Pyrenees

West Highland White Terrier

GIVE HIM ALL THE WATER HE CAN DRINK, AT TIMES
ON THE SCHEDULE. DOGS CRAVE FRESH WATER,
AS PROVEN BY "FRITZ" ABOVE.

DEODORIZING THE AREA

Catching your dog in the act—Since it would be useless to snap a picture and take your dog to court with it, you must find another means of conveying to him what is expected. He must be watched constantly. Keep him in whatever room you are in, and let him drag a piece of clothesline about three to four feet long. This will facilitate his easy removal from a favorite retreat under the couch or behind the bathroom bowl, and will allow you a handle enabling prompt transference to newspapers. When you see your dog trying to make in an undesignated area, yell NO loudly, and lead him with the clothesline, right onto the papers. When he finishes making on the papers, praise him. The contrast between NO and praise, shows your dog what is expected of him and where. If he still does not make on the papers, then just watch closely again.

The next time he attempts elimination in the wrong place, yell NO again, and quickly lead him back on the papers. Repeat this process over and over until the mistakes are eliminated. Do not hit your dog, or rub his nose in it, or yell SHAME. These are all exercises in futility. Continue to deodorize all mistakes with the aforementioned product, and do not show your dog the exasperation you are bound to feel at times in this training process. He will sense your weakness and use it against you. Also, do not shake or throw a rattle can at your dog as a correction. We would not want paper training accomplished at the sacrifice of the dog's personality, where he would be made neurotic and afraid of loud noises for the rest of his life.

During the night, and when you cannot be with your puppy, you must confine him to a small room or part of a room with a gate enclosure, so that he can see out and doesn't become claustrophobic. He will not be

GATE ENCLOSURE FOR CONFINING
PUPPY OVERNIGHT OR WHEN YOU
ARE OUT. SAME TYPE GATE USED
FOR PAPER TRAINING
AND HOUSEBREAKING

excessively anxious, because he can see out. The kitchen is probably the best place, because you have a tile floor that can easily be deodorized. Never confine on a carpeted area. It is much more difficult to remove the scent, and more attractive for him to make on. When you are out you may place him in a small room, perhaps again the kitchen, and cover one half of the room with newspapers. Any mistakes found upon your return that are not on the newspapers, should be deodorized immediately. Do not yell NO to your dog upon returning home. He will not know what he is being corrected for. Just put a clothesline on him and watch him. *Never leave anything on your dog's neck when you are not home.*

Do not bother to correct your dog for making off the papers, even if only two or three minutes have passed. Just clean up the mistake and begin watching him again. Your dog can only understand a correction when he is caught in the act. He must only be corrected at that time.

RUNNING AWAY—

To curtail your dog's nomadic inclinations, something unpleasant has to happen as he goes through the door. This can take the form of silent corrections, in which, to your dog, you would appear to have had no act of participation. Let the dog drag a 15-foot clothesline. Every time he tries to go through the front door, which should be propped open, give a strong, silent jerk on the clothesline. Then turn away and pretend that you had nothing to do with what he just felt. You can and should build up the distractions in this area so that your dog will be most solidly convinced that unpleasant things happen to him when he crosses the threshold without authorization. The only time your dog should go through the door, is when you tell him to by the words OKAY, COME, or HEEL. The greater the number of small children you have and the more heavily trafficked the doors are, what with going to school, returning, and running back and forth into the backyard with their friends, the more essential it is to administer consistent and firm corrections. You must be sure your dog does not run out into the street and get run over, or go into a neighbor's yard and wreak havoc, or bite someone who tries to catch him, or take a reluctant trip to the dog pound, which will require you to retrieve him and pay a fine to boot.

The way to build up distractions, is to have one member of the household strategically located to administer the silent leash correction. This should preferably be the husband or wife. Then have some of the small fry walk in and out, leaving the door propped open. Give the dog every opportunity to make a mistake.

Have some of the children run in and out with their friends, causing an even greater distraction, while leaving the door open all the time. Alternate with husband and wife walking through the door, alone and with the children, then running back and forth. Try leaving the door open with no one around except the adult who will make the correction. Have one of the children go around to the front door and ring the bell. Open the door, while your mate is ready with a leash correction should it be necessary. All this progressive distraction and the accompanying correction should make your dog thoroughly convinced of the futility of running out the door. Enlist the cooperation of all family members until the testing period is over. Don't allow your children to run in and out of doors without first telling you, so that you can stand ready for enforcement. The more consistency used in this initial testing period, the quicker and more secure will be the results. For those of you who find it harder to control small children than your dog, put an auxiliary lock high up on back and front doors, so that children will need you to open doors for them, thereby retaining control over the situation.

The leash correction can be administered from ten to 15 feet away and should consist of a strong backward jerk that will often send the dog flipping back and over on his behind. A little gentle tug won't do the trick. It will be ignored, and his main pursuit, discovering the great outdoors, will continue.

Making your dog sit and stay on command will not work. Dogs best learn something that they themselves have made a decision about. If your dog decides that unpleasant things happen every time he attempts the Charge of the Light Brigade, he will make the right decision, thereby acceding to your wishes without realizing it. Obedience training, both on and off leash, will also help to make this correction more solid and lasting.

With consistency, the 15-foot line can gradually be shortened to as little as one foot long. This will give the dog a constant reminder of the control over him. After many weeks of effective correction, your dog will be convinced that you can correct him any time he attempts running through the door, no matter how short the dragging line. The effectiveness of the preconditioning will carry beyond your actual ability to correct.

Housebreaking the Puppy

Housebreaking implies breaking the dog of relieving himself in the house. A housebroken dog only "makes" outside. Contrarily, a dog that is paper trained eliminates his waste exclusively on papers, in a designated area in the home.

For housebreaking purposes canned dog food is essential, except in rare cases where it causes persistent diarrhea; in that event, packaged, dehydrated food is permissible. Normally, dehydrated packaged burgers, or other dry-packaged food, will make the dog drink large quantities of water, creating the urge to urinate constantly. Keep the dog on canned food, with some kind of cereal or meal mixed in. (See diet chart for ratio of meat to meal.) Water should be restricted by time but not by quantity. At the times designated on the schedule, the dog should be allowed as much water as he wants, but only at those times. He is always taken out right after eating, or watering. Keep him out for five to ten minutes, not longer, during this housebreaking period. You want him to know what he is out for. No half-hour romps around the block, which will only confuse the issue. If he doesn't make in that time, fine; bring him in and *watch him.*

A dog over six months of age would be put on a similar schedule. Let him eat twice a day, eliminating the middle meal, but keeping the water schedule that has him going out about every three to 3½ hours. With the feeding and walking, confining overnight and when you can't be with him, catching him in the act and deodorizing the area, the dog will be housebroken in about two weeks.

DIET

AGE	SIZE OF DOG	MEAL	MEAT (CANNED)
weaning to 3 months (4 meals a day)	Small breeds	1/4 cup	1/4—1/2 can
	Medium breeds	1/3 cup	1/2 can
	Large breeds	1/2 cup	1/2—3/4 can
	Very large breeds	1/2—3/4 cup	3/4 can
3 to 6 months (3 meals a day)	Small breeds	1/2 cup	1/2—3/4 can
	Medium breeds	3/4 cup	3/4 can
	Large breeds	3/4 cup	1 can
	Very large breeds	1½ cups	1—1¾ can
over 6 months (2 meals a day)	Small breeds	1/2 cup	1/2—3/4 can
	Medium breeds	3/4—1 cup	3/4—1¼ cans
	Large breeds	2 cups	1½—2½ cans
	Very large breeds	2—4 cups	2¼—5 cans

THE SCHEDULE

Feedings and walks, three-months-old eating three times a day. Food left down ten mintues only.
7:55 First thing in the morning, fast walk to urinate.
8:00 Food and water
8:10 Walk (5 to 10 minutes on leash, only to make)
11:30 Food and water
11:40 Walk
3:30 Food and water (last solid food of the day)
3:40 Walk
7:00 Water and walk
9:30 Water and walk
11:30 Walk (no water)
　　For dogs six months and older, the 11:30 AM feeding can be eliminated. The last solid food will have to come out at the 11:00 PM walk (approximately six hours after eating); you will be producing an empty dog and, if no water is given after 9:30, a dry dog also. At all other times, between walks, the dog should be watched closely. He should be in

whatever room you are in, and should be dragging three to four feet of clothesline knotted on a bolt snap and attached to his collar. This will give you a handle with which to grab the dog if he starts to make a mistake in the house. When this occurs, yell the word NO and drag him right outside to finish making. As he makes, praise him and bring him back into the house, continuing to watch him. If he doesn't go outside, within five to ten minutes, bring him back in the house and continue watching him. The dog should not go outside to run around and have fun during the housebreaking period. It will create confusion in his mind and delay housebreaking results. Always have him dragging the clothesline when you are able to watch him—if you have to spend time looking for leash and collar, by the time you get them on him he won't know for what he is being corrected or taken outside. Also, don't correct him unless you catch him in the act. Should you be distracted sometime and a mistake occur, firmly resist the temptation to scream and scold and rub his nose in it. Just clean it up and forget about it.

For times when you are not able to watch your dog or to be with him, such as during the night or on a short shopping trip, the dog must be confined. This consists of using two gates to confine the dog in a space not much larger than he is himself. The dog will not make if he has to lie in it; this is his introduction to learning to control himself. Gates are the preferred method of restricting your dog to a small area. The confinement is very close without the dog feeling alienated from the household and smothered by high walls, as in a small bathroom with the door shut. He is able to look out through the gate and feel he is a part of the action, while learning to restrain himself. Should he make a mistake, he will be wearing it. If the area of confinement is too large, it is possible for him to make in one area and lie down and sleep in another, and this he will do. Confinement should be on a hard tile floor that can be deodorized thoroughly. An absorbent rug is much more attractive to a dog and can never be completely deodorized. He tends to make less on a smooth, hard surface.

Your dog should be able to control his bodily functions for eight hours by 3½ months of age, and certainly for an hour or two as you go marketing or to visit a friend. Don't let your pet get in the habit of signaling to you when he would like to go out. Some dogs will assume the role of a cuckoo clock, squawking every hour on the hour. You can easily be fooled into thinking this is a legitimate request that would result in bladder splatter if not indulged promptly. What you don't know is that a dog can always squeeze out a few impressive drops once he has discovered that this is the way to get out for some fun and frolic. If this particular ploy is allowed to blossom into a full-time routine, you may come to feel like a member of the volunteer fire brigade, constantly on call, ready to ease the plight of a doggie in distress.

Some dogs will continue to eliminate even after you yell NO and start dragging them outside. Don't let this deter you. Drag him completely outside, even if there is nothing left. Then praise him, GOOD BOY, and back in the house again. This will end the training exercise on a positive note. You have won, even though he did dribble his excrement all over your rug and down the front stairs. Remember, to the victor belong the spoils. Had you stopped short of getting him outside, he would have defeated you and the housebreaking would take longer. Ideally, you should try to catch your dog as he starts walking in circles, and startle him with a loud NO before he begins to eliminate.

Confinement, watching the dog, catching the dog in the act, and the feeding-walking schedule should housebreak a dog in about two weeks. In that length of time, the dog will be making once or twice in the house for the entire week, but things will be pretty well under control as soon as the whole routine is underway. A liquid deodorizer such as Nilodor should be used in a very strong solution of 15 drops to three cups of water. This mixture should be stored in a jar and used over and over again as needed. No commercial bleaches, pine cleaners, or sprays will work, because even if you can't smell the odor any more, your dog certainly will (his nose is seven times more sensitive than a human's). As long as he can smell his past mistakes, his super nose will lead him back to these spots to repeat the experience. Nilodor has a very clean fresh smell that does not mask odors but actually eliminates them.

If you are a business couple and no one is home during the day, housebreaking will take longer. It can take a month to six weeks and even more, because during the day you can't confine the dog in a very small spot. Having the run of a larger area like the kitchen, he would be able to make in one end of the room and sleep in another, without wearing his mistake. Ground gained when you are home would be lost when you aren't. Otherwise, all else on the schedule would remain the same. It is a good idea to walk the dog as soon as you get home, before feeding. This walk should be very short, approximately two minutes, like the first walk in the morning. People who complain that they walk their dog for an hour outside and that he makes upon returning, are allowing this to happen by having far too lengthy walks and then not watching the dog when he returns.

If he isn't allowed to make in the house because you are watching him, and won't make in confinement because he doesn't want to wear it, then there are only two choices left: make outside, or bust. We haven't witnessed any explosions yet. If done properly and thoroughly, this routine will housebreak any dog in about two weeks.

In cases where walking a dog is not possible, for whatever reason, paper training must be chosen as the alternative to housebreaking. Paper training means that the dog will make on papers placed in one particular area inside the house.

Paper training is similar to housebreaking in that the schedule of feedings remains the same, but instead of walking him outside, he is put on the papers. The papers, in the initial stages, take up the entire floor of a small room. later the area is narrowed down to as little as a foot square, depending on the size of the dog.

Catching your dog in the act is the same, except that you will be dragging your dog to the papers and praising him when he makes on them.

The confinement area will start off being an entire room with the papers. Instead of closing the door, a gate should be used to confine him in the room. After five days and a few mistakes off the papers, remove the papers covering half the room and deodorize the exposed area with a very strong solution of Nilodor. All other areas in the home where mistakes occur should be thoroughly deodorized as well.

Besides being placed in the room with the papers as a correction each time he tries to make elsewhere in the house, the dog will be confined in that room at night. As fewer mistakes are made, usually in about five days to a week, the dog will not require overnight confinement anymore. The dog must have access to this room at all times, and will only be gated in when no one is able to watch him, such as when you are asleep or out. Need we remind you that every time the dog makes on the papers he should be lavishly praised.

Paper training should be used as an alternative to housebreaking, not as an augmentative routine. The fewer your dog's choices, the more successful will be the training.

73

CORRECT EQUIPMENT FOR TRAINING YOUR PUPPY

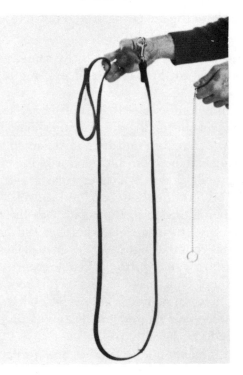

Puppy Basic Obedience

(three-to-six-months old)

There is a need to establish communication between you and your puppy. Even though you cannot be very demanding of your dog, so far as expecting him to respond to complicated commands, you must retain enough control over him to be able to live together amicably until his brain matures, at about five months of age, and he is able to understand what will be expected of him.

The equipment you will need to begin basic obedience training with your pup consists of a metal chain-type collar and a six-foot leather or canvas-web training leash. This same equipment should be used for his daily housebreaking walks, to familiarize him with it, and to eliminate any fear that may carry over into the obedience training. Puppy obedience should be worked for 15 minutes a day, no longer. Some pups can only tolerate short training sessions; their attention wanders or they get very nervous. For this type, five-minute segments, two or three times daily, will work better than one 15-minute session.

COME—

You need some way of mobilizing your dog into action. If you can't get him to walk with you, he can't be taught the SIT, STAY, or any other command. The word OKAY is used as a release, to start the dog moving. This is followed by the dog's name, and then the command COME. That combination of words will enable you to start the dog walking with you on leash. It is not an exercise in heeling; it is a prelude to the command HEEL, which will be taught in obedience when your dog comes of age and his mental faculties can handle this more complicated training. The COME command will sound like this, OKAY! JOE—COME.

The first obedience routine will consist of walking back and forth in a room and stopping approximately every six feet. Do not start this training out of doors where distractions will be intensified, making it very difficult for your pup to concentrate. Try to work in a minimally furnished room

75

PROPER WAY
TO INSTALL
CHAIN COLLAR

"OKAY!
PUPPY,
COME"

where you will not be tripping over table legs or bumping into couches. In addition to your safety and comfort, there is another important consideration. Your pup can draw emotional support if he is allowed to lean on or get under or even near tables, chairs, or other furniture. Work him in the middle of the room, as far from temptation as possible. You are initiating your dog into moving with you, not defying an obstacle course.

In many homes, training the family pet becomes a joint family venture and a favorite spectator sport for the children and their little friends. Cheers from the crowd and sage remarks from the peanut gallery do not a good training session make. Resist the temptation to make a public spectacle of yourself and a fiasco of the training sessions. Let your advisors confine their talents to reviewing the state of their bedrooms or the serious shortage of helpful little hands at the kitchen sink.

You will begin placing your dog on sits immediately, with the first training session.

SIT—

You should be walking back and forth with your pup, giving the command, OKAY, JOE—COME. When you stop, place your dog on a sit by pushing down on the dog's rear end with your left hand, while drawing up smoothly on the leash with your right hand. Say the word SIT only once. As your dog is forced to sit, you will praise him, GOOD BOY. As the command SIT is given, the dog is physically pushed into the sit position. *Only one command is given.* This should be repeated for some five to ten minutes every day for about a week. After that time your puppy should be able to sit for you on command, especially in the house, without distractions. Never reward him with food or he will not work without it. Your physical and vocal praise will be his complete reward.

After your puppy has been placed on sits for about a week, he should be sitting most, if not all, of the time on your command. If he will not sit all of the time, you can now start correcting him. It is safe to assume he knows what you want. If he refuses to heed your command to sit, you can now correct by giving a slight jerk on the leash, accompanied by the word NO, and then praise if he sits. The proper leash correction consists of a quick jerk and release movement, not an extended hanging. If he is still not sitting after the NO correction, give another SIT command. If he still does not sit, give another correction and then the SIT command again. You will keep this up as long as neccessary, until you win out, alternating the correction with a new SIT command. Do not go back to placing your

PRAISE, "GOOD BOY"

SIT CORRECTION, USING THE WORD "NO"

SIT PLACEMENT

78

dog on sits, once you have decided that he knows it. You will only correct in the manner described above.

If you are wondering how hard you should jerk your dog when correcting him, the answer is simple. His actions will tell you. If he refuses to sit after a few corrections, it means you are correcting too lightly. If he sits after a correction, then you know it was hard enough. The greatest cruelty a misguided handler can inflict on a dog is an ineffective under-correction. Undercorrecting encourages further resistance and the need for many more corrections, which all add up to a lot of unnecessary pain for your dog. The greatest kindness is a good, hard, effective correction that does the job the first time, ending the need for any further corrections. The biggest injustice to a dog is dispensed by the misguided "kind" person who is too good-hearted to jerk his dog. This same kind person, three months later, gives the uncontrollable dog away to the dog pound to be killed. Such a person is a dog's greatest enemy. Make sure you do not emulate him—for your dog's sake.

SITTING ON COMMAND

STAY —

The stay is begun only after your dog will reliably sit on command for you. When your dog is sitting, hold your left hand extended in front of him, slowly moving it toward his face, and say the word STAY only once. Hesitate for two or three seconds and then praise him. On the next stop, once your dog has sat, give the STAY command acompanied by the hand signal. It is important to note that only one STAY command and signal will be given. After about five repetitions, give the STAY command when he sits, and then step a half-foot back away from the dog. Return quickly to the dog's side and praise him. The stays should be so short at the beginning that the dog doesn't have a chance to break. This will end the routine on a positive note, with your dog being praised. Next will follow a repetition, for five times, of the SIT and STAY commands, stepping back a half-foot. On the sixth attempt, give the STAY command and step back away from your dog about four feet. Immediately drop your hand, return to your dog and praise him. That is enough for the first day.

Gradually increase the distance between you and the dog as you back away to the full six-foot length of the leash. Always return quickly before your dog has a chance to break. Correspondingly increase the time until, after about a week, your dog can sit and stay for half a minute at the full length of the six-foot leash.

After an additional week of practice, your dog should be able to stay for a minute to a minute and a half, despite slight distractions. If your dog breaks the stay by getting up, the correction should be NO, with a slight jerk on the leash, from the full six feet away, and a repetition of the commands SIT and STAY, together with the correct hand signal. Don't wait till your pup runs to you; try to correct as he breaks the stay. Should he get far, drag him back quickly to the point where he was first told to stay, and give a new SIT and STAY command with the hand signal. Leave your dog again. Should he get up and break the stay upon your return, he gets the usual NO correction with a jerk on the leash and a repetition of the commands SIT and STAY with the proper hand signal. Continue this until you can return to his side and praise him without his breaking. Moving slowly, when returning to your dog, will help him to hold the stay. Hesitate about three seconds after returning to the dog's side, before praising him. In this way you will be teaching him to wait for your praise instead of using your mere physical proximity, when you return, as an automatic release for himself. This hesitation before praising will make the stays much more solid.

HAND SIGNAL FOR "STAY"

OUT IN FRONT, TENSION ON LEASH

OUT IN FRONT, RELAXED TENSION
ON LEASH

Do not expect too much of a three- or four-month-old puppy, and don't put him in severe distractions where you will be forced to correct frequently. This will make him fearful of the obedience to come later when he will be mentally equipped to handle more intense training.

Once the dog will respond to your SIT and STAY commands, you can begin walking him outside. You will have more control over the outside puller. He can be commanded to SIT and STAY at five-foot intervals. This will force your dog to pay more attention to you than to the distractions in the street. This is a refreshing objective, as any flustered puppy owner can attest.

This early phase of obedience is not to be confused with heeling, which will come later. These few commands, and the basic attitude of respect you have established between your puppy and yourself, will suffice until he is six months of age and mentally able to absorb the increased rigors of the formal obedience training.

NO—

Only one word is going to be used as a correction to convey your disapproval to your dog for some specific wrongdoing. That word is NO. NO should be used with a simultaneous leash correction that consists of a jerk on the leash with an immediate release. Eventually, NO will also be used verbally only sometimes, after your dog has established a strong association with the accompanying physical correction and there is no longer any leash or line on him. Do not command your dog DOWN for jumping up on you, or at times when he momentarily becomes a giraffe to sneak a tasty morsel from the table. Use the word NO for all these negative acts. You should also refrain from lecturing him on proper table manners, or on etiquette when meeting people at the door, such as, "You know Poochie, that mommy gets very angry when you take things from the table," or "It's not very nice of you to jump on Grandma when she comes to visit." Your dog needs simplification. He wants to know the ground rules. He welcomes consistency because then he will not have to suffer an unjust correction from you when you are in a bad mood and scream at him for doing something you have let him get away with dozens of other times.

NO is a very simple logical word to use for all negative behavior. It should be accompanied by the proper voice inflection, authoritative as opposed to coy and condescending. And you don't want to go to the opposite extreme and utter a ferocious roar that would turn your dog into a cowering neurotic.

"STAY" ON FULL 6 FEET OF LEASH

NEW "STAY" COMMAND

"STAY" CORRECTION

RENEWED "STAY" FROM 6 FEET

A very important aspect of the NO correction is the praise that should always follow when he stops what you are correcting. If there is no contrast between correction and praise, your dog will not know what he was corrected for. By giving your dog this consistent contrast between the correction on the one hand, and the praise on the other, you set the stage for him to make a choice. If you are consistent, he will make the correct choice.

OKAY—

Just as NO is used as a correction for all negative behavior, OKAY will be used as a release from work or training. Your dog is not a mind reader so don't expect him to realize when a lesson is over without a verbal release. Likewise, do not expect him to start heeling or sitting simply because you pick up the leash and have it in mind that he should do so. Your dog must be initiated into each training session with a command such as Dream, HEEL, or Whitey, COME, and released from work with the word OKAY expressed joyously, as you simultaneously throw down the leash and so convey to your pet that he is released from control.

Since you are in the driver's seat as to when a training session starts and finishes, the weight of responsibility is also upon you not to overwork your dog to the point of irritability or exhaustion. Several short periods of five to ten minutes are much better than one hour-long marathon.

STEALING FROM THE TABLE

"STAY" SIGNAL
OUT OF DOORS

PRAISE, "GOOD BOY"
ON RETURN FROM
"STAY"

RETURN AND
PRAISE
FROM "STAY" COMMAND

STAY" OUTSIDE
 N FULL 6 FEET
F LEASH

I'M AFRAID TO OBEDIENCE TRAIN HIM, I HEARD IT COULD BREAK HIS SPIR

Obedience Training

(at six months of age)

In beginning basic obedience, it is extremely helpful if we first can assess knowledgeably our own dog's basic personality traits. This is because, in following each essential step for learning a specific command, it is almost always necessary to deviate from standard procedure to some extent to encompass a wide spectrum of offbeat reactions to the norm. The scale of basic behavioral classifications runs the personality gamut from overfriendly to high-strung, to normal-average, to aloof, to shy-afraid, to fear-biter, and ultimately to aggressive. A dog can and will travel through these various strata of personality aberrations beginning with superfriendliness and ending favorably by maintaining a normal-average response, or ending unfavorably by lapsing into aggression. You can make an overfriendly dog turn aggressive, but you can also nurture a normal response in a heretofore aggressive dog. All these refinements are possible with knowledge.

If, the first time you correct your dog, he bites you on the butt; or, as you attempt to correct your gregarious pet, he climbs the leash like a fireman and ends up in your arms; or you start heeling your dog and he rolls over on his back and obstinately refuses to walk, leaving you dragging what resembles a lifeless ham hock across the pavement; or you start placing your dog on sits and he responds by curtsying with his front legs and rearing up with his rear, you might quite rapidly jump to the conclusion that obedience training for your particular pet is hopeless, or that what we are advising is a crock of cheese-wiz. If we only guided you in the ideal corrections for the logical responses from the ideal dog, you would be in for a plethora of frustrating times with your pet. Fortunately for us, as well as the dog, there are very few dogs that are actually untrainable. Some of the extreme reasons why a dog may be untrainable would be if he suffered brain damage, or if he were so gravely beaten as a pup that he turns a deaf ear to any disciplinary activity; or, in the case of a guard dog, if he were misappropriately agitated (as many of them are), so the wrong training could never be unlearned.

You have dual objectives at the outset of training. First is to define properly and honestly which basic category of behavior your dog justly belongs in, and, secondly, to refine and tailor the obedience so that the dog will ultimately gravitate toward the norm, regardless of which end of the spectrum he strated at. The primary value of a professional dog trainer lies in the fact that he has the acuity to zero in on personality deviations and behavioral problems, and can quickly diminish or negate those problems through his skill in accurate diagnosis. His brain is a diagnostic center and he can adjust the pulse of your dog's psychological engine, refining it for peak efficiency.

We will start by describing the normal-average dog. This dog has probably been in your family since puppyhood. You have most likely not hit him or thrown things at or near him for minor transgressions. He has had a healthy upbringing, untainted by yelling or abuse or irrational behavior on your part or from any member of the family. He has not been teased unmercifully by little children of left tied up in a cold garage or a wet basement. The normal-average dog could be any breed, but probably is not among the hunting or northern group. He is usually calm and friendly. Your praise is his motivation for doing things. He does not obey out of fear, but from a genuine desire to please you and gain your acceptance. He cares what you think about him and enjoys your attention. He is not overly excitable with noises, doorbells, or strange people. Behavior is moderate in all areas. He has a well-rounded, stable personality and is the ideal dog for companionship as well as training.

The overfriendly dog takes on like an epileptic frenzy whenever the doorbell rings. He paces and flys around the room, looking like a sea captain trying to prevent your kitchen from capsizing. He gives your guests an unsolicited facial and tries to soul kiss with anyone who is the least bit receptive. His bodily calisthenics resemble a giant springloaded yo-yo that is perpetually overwound. He is the bane of all well-dressed guests, driving many to equal maneuvers around your living room and entrance way in an effort to escape his affection. This embarrassing display is usually stopped by the owner engineering the dog into the bathroom or an enclosed porch. It takes an extremely long time for the overfriendly dog to calm down, if he does so at all. Where the overfriendly dog is large-size and he jumps up on small children with his paws in their faces, knocking them into walls and off their feet, serious injuries could result. He is literally killing them with his love.

The high-strung dog is an extension of the overfriendly dog. He is very nervous and up-tight. He worries about every strange noise. He is likely to react very severely to firecrackers or thunder. You may see visible shaking of his body; the heartbeat may become more rapid. He may try to crawl onto your lap for comfort and security or may cower in a corner away from everyone, shivering. He may whine a lot or howl from fear and anxiety. Colitis is sometimes a related problem, causing momentary diarrhea or acid indigestion. The hair on his back could rise, and he might make a mistake and nip or bite from worry or fear. He overreacts when people come to call. His bark goes far beyond alerting you to someone's presence. He will run around excessively, and often gives your guests a feeling of discomfort at his presence. His behavior makes people reticent about extending their hands to pet him. He might be reacting to you, his master, and his home environment or he may be reacting to what is inherent in his personality. Recognizing why he is the way he is would be helpful. But it is more important to realize that he behaves in a certain manner, and thereby correctly categorize him for purposes of training efficiency and effectiveness.

The aloof dog is a "cool-cat." He jives with his own pleasures, attempting to do "his thing" as often as possible. When you attempt to persuade him to do your thing, he responds with an attitude that equates with a belligerent child protesting "make me." He doesn't work for your praise, only from fear that you will enforce your demands. This rebel is not a dumb bunny, as everyone usually thinks. He is smart enough to avoid doing anything that is not absolutely forced upon him. This shouldn't surprise you, because you doubtless know several people who behave in much the same way. The aloof dog can be very lovable at times when nothing is required of him, or he may remain undemonstrative all of the time, sashaying through the house with an invisible shield of ice cubes. He can be stubborn and very hard to housebreak. He is as unmanageable as hair before the cream rinse. Be honest, and willing to put your dog in this category if he deserves it. To deny the truth will cause problems all along the way. You will seriously impede training if you follow procedures suited to another type of dog.

The shy-afraid dog may have been brought to your home as an adolescent, or even as an adult dog. When a dog was not in your care for a considerable portion of his life, beyond the eight to ten weeks from birth to complete weaning from its mother, many unfavorable events can have occurred over which you have no control. These events could severely warp your dog's personality. He may have been abused in any number of ways by people entrusted with his care and well-being. These formative months of a dog's life have a lasting influence on his mature behavior. You may be the second or third owner of this dog. In spite of the belief of many people that a dog has absolutely no trouble adjusting to new owners and new environments, this supposition is not true. Many dogs have a great sense of loyalty and emotional attachment to their owners. They often have difficulty in transferring their affections from one owner to another. Compounding the problem even more is the fact that many dogs do not go directly from one household into another. The interim period is often spent in an animal shelter, which at best is a very cold and unpleasant place for a dog. When he does arrive in new family surroundings, he has already been somewhat tainted by his feelings of rejection and alienation, and will take some time before feeling secure in his new situation. The shy-afraid dog has most likely been dealt a rough hand, somewhere along the way, and your patience and understanding will go a long way toward overcoming his problems.

The fear-biter can be the high-strung dog, the shy-afraid, or a combination of both. He acts aggressively at certain times. This is the type of dog that appears vicious and aggressive when at his master's side, but when directly confronted alone he may back down. His courage also gets a boost when he is surrounded by the protective cover and safety of couches, tables, etc. A favorite pastime is attacking people who are trying to leave, or people who merely stand up, touch certain objects, or intrude upon certain hallowed ground. This dog looks for an excuse to justify a bite, which his sick mind readily rationalizes. He especially looks for people who are afraid, thriving on their fear, which intensifies his aggression. His target areas are usually your rump, ankle, or the back of a leg. This is because the fear-biter rarely attacks head on. He generally prefers making your back his target. He specializes in apparently unprovoked surprise attacks that his mind has justified. His aggression could be a result of poor breeding; abusive treatment to correct problems such as housebreaking, jumping, etc; and erratic or irrational behavior on the part of family members. He sees everything out of proportion. An attempt to pet him is often misconstrued as an aggressive, threatening gesture. The fear-biter progresses in stages from barking to nipping to biting, and gets worse as he is allowed to get away with it. He is overly defensive and is more apt to make a mistake than any other category than the aggressive dog. The fear-biter is most dangerous to strangers and, in advanced stages, can be a danger even to his owners and their family members. He can be reclaimed by honest evaluation in placing him in this category, and by proper handling methods especially suited to his particular problems.

The aggressive dog is the most dangerous and potentially volcanic of all the personality categories. He is perfectly willing to bite almost anyone at any time. His presence can be a living nightmare. Every dog,

THE AGGRESSIVE DOG

in his own mind, has to justify a bite, and the aggressive dog will bite on the flimsiest of provocations. He is often loaded with idiosyncrasies, and if he decides that you are threatening his sense of well-being by standing up, or blowing your nose, or reaching down to pet him, he will spring into action to convey his displeasure. The aggressive dog's personality may stem from overpermissiveness, or from extremely abusive treatment, such as harsh beatings or teasing from children. Or he may be a product of poor breeding. This damage could have been caused before you got your dog, or your own behavior may be the sole cause of his aggression. If you determine that you are the one to blame, then honestly evaluate what things you are doing wrong and stop them immediately. Start a positive change by beginning the obedience program. This will serve to control the negative behavior through positive action.

However, it is most dangerous for anyone, sometimes even the owner, to work an aggressive dog. You cannot really afford errors in judgment. Indulging yourself in a barrage of excuses is also harmful since you must come to terms with what your dog is and what you are capable of doing to handle this problem and change him. If you feel that this is a challenge beyond your capabilities, consult a professional dog trainer. Don't bury your head in the sand, because what's left exposed is still open to attack. If your dog passes some of the preliminary tests at the beginning of the following obedience chapters, chances are you can work out his problems with the help of this book. Should he fail these preliminary tests, then professional guidance is positively called for. Don't chance death or serious injury to yourself or other innocent

91

people, and don't expose your dog to the possible ultimate necessity of having to be destroyed. We are so conditioned to getting rid of things when they no longer please us that this attitude is often carried over to living things. Even if your dog is aggressive, and you feel you cannot handle him, he is not hopeless. Most aggressive dogs can be brought under control by the proper methods, that being the use of this book or the services of a professional trainer.

The equipment used for obedience training is very simple but very important. Do not skimp on the proper equipment by trying to make do with what you already have. The correct collar and leash will probably cost you less than the price of this book. If it isn't worth the investment, then you shouldn't be training your dog.

A metal chain collar, as shown in the accompanying photo, will be needed; this chain collar has two rings, one at each end. The collars come in various lengths from eight to 32 inches, in two-inch progressions, and in some five different weights of links, advancing in thickness from very fine to extra heavy as the length is increased. Try to buy the thickest collar for your particular size; there will be added strength and much less chance of breakage.

Place the chain around your dog's neck by slippng one ring through the other and forming a loop like the letter P with the chain. With your dog facing you, slip the P over his head. When worn correctly, with the dog on your left side, the collar will release immediately after tightening. But when put on backwards it will tighten and not release, choking your dog.

STRAP COLLAR AND
NYLON CHOKE COLLAR

PROPER EQUIPMENT

CORRECT COLLAR INSTALLATION

WRONG COLLAR INSTALLATION

To determine the correct size of chain for your dog, place it around his neck. There should be two inches of overhang. More than this could cause him to get snared when he drags it around without the leash, and less than this would be too tight going over his ears. You would also have too little slack to tighten effectively for corrections. The chain collar can be worn all the time, so long as it fits correctly.

As for what not to use, do not try to work with a strap collar. This has a fixed size once it is on the dog and offers no correction features. Strap collars are good if you must occasionally tie up your dog. The very thick strap collars are used in guard work. For both of these purposes, the fact that the collar does not tighten, can be used to advantage. You may be thinking of sparing your dog excess punishment by using a strap collar for obedience training instead of a chain collar. This book is written with the thought of inflicting as little pain as possible. That is why training with a chain collar is mandatory. True, the chain collar inflicts more shocking pain, but it corrects quickly and effectively, encouraging no further resistance. The strap collar will produce little or no correction, but only a nagging pull that encourages resistance and that actually twists and damages the dog's neck. Hard, effective corrections are necessary to train a dog; which renders the strap collar ineffective. Therefore the only intelligent choice is the chain collar.

Another type of collar is called a show choke, which is a fancy version of the choke chain. It tightens only partially and is ineffective for obedience work. There is also a variety of the choke collar called a fur saver. This is a choke chain made of rectangular links. It may save the fur at the cost of the dog. You cannot get effective corrections with it. Some of the fur will fly in training, but this is only temporary and needn't cause any alarm.

A desirable type of collar that you will be able to use later on is called the nylon choke collar. It looks just like the metal choke chain, except that it is made of nylon fabric. This collar will not chop up fur as much as the metal collar will, and can be used after your dog is well established in his obedience patterns. Part of the effectiveness of the metal chain collar lies in its ability to make noise as well as to provide more stringent physical corrections than the nylon collar. Which is why the use of the nylon choke collar must be deferred until your dog works well for you on the metal collar.

I would like to comment about spike or pronged collars that are sold indiscriminately, by pet shops, to people whose big dogs pull them down the street. A spike collar, contrary to popular belief, does not dig into the dog's neck. It corrects by pinching the skin when the prongs come together. Jerking on the collar, makes the prongs tighten. This causes about three times the punishment of a chain-collar correction. Casual use of the spike collar can cause irreparable damage to your dog. The spike collar will be used in extreme cases, by a professional trainer, and should never be used by any person on his own dog.

The proper training leash should be a six-foot canvas web, or preferably leather, lead with a bolt snap on one end and a securely finished loop on the other end. The leather leash is the most durable, but also the most costly. Do not buy those brightly colored plastic leashes of various short lengths; they are useless for training purposes. An equally worthless bit of equipment is the metal chain leash. Corrections made with this leash will hurt your hands more than your dog. Some suppliers make it very hard for you to train your dog, by not having the proper equipment. Don't expect to find it in your local supermarket. Persevere and you will find it. The six-foot length is absolutely necessary to provide an average proper distance between you and your dog on stays. It also allows the proper amount of slack to catch him on right-about turns. There are ten- to 50-foot tracking leads and leashes available, but these have very specific applications and are useless for obedience training of any kind.

THE BEST WAY TO USE THE INFORMATION IN THIS SECTION OF THE BOOK IS FIRST TO READ THE TRAINING PROCEDURE AS APPLIED TO THE NORMAL-AVERAGE DOG. THEN, IF YOUR DOG FALLS INTO ONE OF THE OTHER SIX CATEGORIES, REFER TO THE METHODS OUTLINED THEREAFTER FOR YOUR PARTICULAR TYPE OF DOG.

THE ATTENTION-GETTER

THE FIRST DAY

The Normal-average Dog—The first day's training session should begin with the six-foot web training leash on and the choke chain around your dog's neck in the correct fashion: make the letter P with the chain and slip it over his head with him facing you. The dog is now attired for serious training sessions.

Your dog can be on either side of you. Put your right-hand thumb through the end loop of the leash. Close your fist on the leash. Clasp your left hand over your right hand. You are holding the leash at its end and the entire six-foot length is between you and your dog. Then, without saying a word to your dog, just start walking. This can be in the backyard, or in front of your house, as long as there are not too many distractions.

THE ATTENTION GETTER

Don't ask his permission, don't beg him, don't say HEEL because he is not heeling yet. Just walk. Walk at a normal pace from one end of your yard to the other, and stop. Once you get there, just relax for about 20 seconds. Look around, ignoring your dog; don't look at him. Then, suddenly, without any warning, start walking back to the other side and continue until you get there.

Your dog may lie down or scream. You have never done this to him before. You have always coaxed and humored him, followed the dictates of his desires, but now you are walking and he is probably being dragged, possibly walking, jumping on you or even attempting to bite you. He might be running in front of you so that you actually fall over him. He could be trying anything to prevent your getting from one point to the other without having his permission or approval. Whatever your pet's ploy, you must continue until you reach your objective, the starting point. Once you get there, take another break of maybe half a minute, then start back to the far side again. Continue walking at a normal pace even if your dog lunges in front of you, or away from you, or screams in frantic indignation. No matter what he does, ignore him. Don't look at him; just continue to walk at a normal pace. If he tangles the leash by stepping on it, let it be that way. Just drag him kicking and screaming across the yard. Once you get to your stopping point, take a half-minute pause, again ignoring your dog. Then start again, back to the other point. Continue this for about 15 minutes, then give your dog a break.

For the break we need a 20-foot clothesline with a bolt snap attached at one end, which makes for quick and easy installation and removal. When you are ready to give your dog his break, first snap on the clothesline, then remove the leash. You should be holding the end of the 20-foot clothesline looped around your thumb. Take off the leash, toss it on the ground in front of your dog, and, in a loud, happy voice, tell him OKAY, THAT'S ALL. Depending on what category your dog is in, you will have different reactions to this apparent release. It is more important what you do, than what he does.

Your dog's reactions may range from taking off at full speed, like a rocket, to just standing near you, looking at you. If he takes off like a rocket, silently turn in the opposite direction, gripping the line tightly with both hands, and run, with equal thrust and speed, away from the dog. When your dog runs out of line, this will cause a terrific impact as he is jerked back forcefully towards you. You should not yell anything at him or communicate verbally with him in any way. All you should do, immediately after the impact, is walk toward your dog. Walking toward him puts back the necessary slack in the clothesline that will be needed for

97

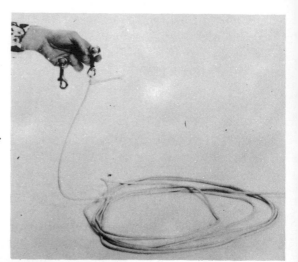

**CLOTHESLINE AND
BOLTSNAP EQUIPMENT**

**CORRECTION ON
CLOTHESLINE**

**STANDING ATTENTIVELY
ON CLOTHESLINE**

98

his next charge. Your dog will probably get up and look at you very puzzled, trying to figure out what happened because this has never occurred before. He will probably make another charge as equally determined as the first. Let him take off and, once again, you should turn and run hard in the opposite direction, producing the same silent, powerful correction. After two of these corrections a lot of dogs are convinced that this rocketlike charge is definitely not a good thing to do. For a few more-determined dogs it may take four, five, or more corrections before the same results are achieved. Your dog is learning that bad things will happen to him if he tries to run away from you. Your dog may learn not to run away after one correction, or after ten corrections, but learn he will if you do your part correctly.

It doesn't matter how many corrections it takes to produce the desired response, but as many as are needed must be provided by you. The ideal response is that your dog will stand near you, looking at you, showing little or no desire to run away. This response is usually achieved in two corrections with most dogs. During the break you should also give your dog the silent treatment. There will be no praise after the correction, and no praise when the dog watches and stays close to you. The dog is not reacting to please you; he is just finding what is safest and most comfortable for him. Lessons learned in this way will last a lifetime.

The above procedures may be frowned upon by some misguided, well-meaning, and very vocal people. These people are the ones who can't stand to see a poor doggie hurt. You may find them leaning over a backyard fence, on the street, hanging out of an open window, or even as part of your own family. Some of their favorite lines are; "You're going to make that dog vicious," "That's no way to treat a dog," or "You'll break that dog's neck." They think they have much better ways of dealing with dogs. They give them cookies and the dogs perform, and this makes them happy. Although these people frown on your cruel, vicious, inhumane training methods, which to them is mistreating your dog, they have no compunction about having your dog destroyed, or given away for housebreaking, chewing, or obedience problems. They don't blink an eye if you tell them your dog got hit by a car, but they scream at you, at the top of their lungs, if they see you jerk your dog with the leash.

You must completely reject and ignore this kind of person if you intend to train your dog successfully. Sooner or later you will probably come across a person such as this. When you do, you will find that no answer is the best answer of all; completely ignoring the stupid remarks and comments is the best procedure you can follow. Directly or indirectly, these people kill hundreds of dogs each year and are, in reality, the worst enemies of all dogs. They should also be yours.

I SAW YOU JERK THAT DOG, YOU MONSTER!

After about a five-minute break, swap the clothesline for the leash and go back again for Round Two of exactly the same routine—noncommunicative walking as you did before. This should last another 15 minutes, again followed by a five-minute break, as outlined above, which will end the session for the first day.

The Overfriendly Dog,
The High-strung Dog,
The Aloof Dog—For all of these dogs, you should follow the same procedure as outlined above for the normal-average dog.

The Shy-afraid Dog—Sometimes, in extreme cases, the shy-afraid dog should be verbally praised for walking. This provides an incentive for him to continue walking and diminishes the need for unpleasant dragging, which is not beneficial to this particular type of dog.

The Fear-biter—will not normally bite you on the attention-getter. If he does make an all-out attack, this may indicate that you have incorrectly classified an aggressive dog as a fear-biter. If such is the case, then go on to the instructions for the aggressive dog. In rare instances the fear-biter may try to bite you. Since he prefers attacking from behind, the attention-getter, with its full six feet of leash, provides him with the opportunity to get behind you, bite, and run a safe six feet away. This differs from an aggressive dog's all-out frontal attack. Biting from behind, and then running away, indicates that you have correctly classified your dog as a fear-biter. In this situation he is an extreme case. To handle his problem, you must limit the freedom of movement that the dog will have on the leash and restrict his opportunity to move behind you and get away from you. This is done by completely bypassing the attention-getter and going right on to heeling, in the next section, which will bring the dog in very close proximity to you. Your dog should be working on about two feet of leash, and will be unable to get behind you for a bite and then run a safe six feet away.

If you have the type of fear-biter who will bite other people but not you, or who just chooses not to bite you, then you can continue with the attention getter as described above, with the five-minute breaks after each 15-minute training session.

The Aggressive Dog—may not like running to the end of the leash and being jerked, with the attendant surprise and discomfort that this correction causes. He may possibly turn around and bite you. With the aggressive dog it is important that he be praised verbally, immediately after a correction. If the aggressive dog runs around and barks or growls or both, continue to walk. Regardless of how obstinate he becomes, continue to walk till you have reached your predetermined stopping point. If he is running alongside of you, jumping and mouthing, or even nipping lightly, do not allow him to deter you. He fully expects that his actions will deter you, and you must prove him wrong. Try to keep your hands away from him. Continue walking, holding both hands together and touching your chest. This position serves best to absorb impacts. It also presents the least threatening posture to your dog and, lastly, it leaves him no protrusive objects to grab on to and bite. Nothing short of an all-out biting attack should stop you from walking. If his bullying tactics are unsuccessful, they will diminish and he will stop. As this occurs he will slowly be changing his attitude toward you and you will be gaining a new respect, making it possible to work the dog and make him a valuable member of the household. If you are able to work your aggressive dog,

101

DRAGGING THE
RELUCTANT DOG

you should work him as described previously, with two 15-minute sessions and the controlled five-minute breaks after each session. If, however, your dog comes on strongly and actually bites you, you have a serious problem requiring the help of a professional trainer. When a dog will bite you for almost no reason at all, neither one of you will last through the more rigid requirements that are part of the rest of the obedience training. A professional dog trainer should be called immediately.

THE SECOND DAY

The Normal-average Dog—The second day's training consists of an exact repetition of the first day's procedure. As you start to walk, you may be pleasantly surprised by your dog's change in attitude. You may find that, as you start to walk, without saying a word to your dog, he is moving at your side. Continue the same described routine for the second day: 15 minutes and a five-minute break, then 15 more minutes, a final five-minute break, and then stop for the day. Make sure your dog hasn't eaten anything for at least three hours prior to each training session.

After each training session, ignore your dog. Don't sympathize with him or play with him, or let anyone else heap condolences upon him, affirming in his mind what a bad, abusive time he had. Keep everyone away from him. Let him be alone, to think over what has just happened. Ignore him for 15 minutes after each training session. Like the first day's procedure, your two 15-minute training sessions should each be followed by the same five-minute breaks on the long clothesline. By the end of the second day your dog should be increasingly attentive. Every time you start to walk he should be moving along with you.

The Overfriendly Dog,
The High-strung Dog—These dogs should be calming down as they are being worked into each consecutive day.

The Aloof Dog—may still be resisting by holding back. He must be dragged and not allowed to bring a halt to the training session by not walking. He must learn that this tactic will avail him nothing. Continue to drag him, possibly even running, and he will soon choose to walk. You must outlast him and be more stubborn than he is.

The Shy-afraid Dog,
The Fear-biter,
The Aggressive Dog—These dogs should be more secure and confident as the days go by. Continue the regular routine as their confidence grows.

THE THIRD DAY

The Normal-average Dog,
The Overfriendly Dog,
The High-strung Dog,
The Aloof Dog,
The Shy-afraid Dog,
The Fear-biter,
The Aggressive Dog—Follow the same procedure as for the second day with all of these dogs.

THE FOURTH DAY

The Normal-average Dog,
The Overfriendly Dog,

The High-strung Dog,
The Aloof Dog,
The Shy-afraid Dog,
The Fear-biter,
The Aggressive Dog—Follow the same procedures as for the second and third days with all of these dogs. By the end of the fourth day's training, your dog, (no matter what his category) should be walking when you walk, stopping when you stop, and paying more attention to you than you have ever thought possible.

THE FIFTH DAY

The Normal-average Dog—We will begin the fifth day's training lesson with the 20-foot-long clothesline that was previously used on the breaks. Discard the six-foot leash for now; you are ready for what we will call "the big surprise." This big surprise will be in the form of a distraction and a correction. The best distractions are the things your dog likes best or goes for most enthusiastically. This could be another dog, a favorite "people playmate," children walking, a cat crossing his path, or any other irresistible force that will make your dog forget about you and charge toward the distraction. In order to be effective, the distraction must be a completely controllable situation. This means that both the distraction and the environment must be controlled. A fenced-in backyard or an isolated park or beach area is preferable to the streets of a heavily trafficked city where all kinds of enticements can suddenly appear, making contact with your dog and nullifying the effectiveness of this lesson. The dog or cat (distraction) must be held on a leash or tied to a fence or post, and not be allowed to make contact with your dog. Children can be enlisted to help you, by walking or running past your dog, but they must follow your instructions closely and not be allowed to touch or pet the dog while they are being used as the distraction. At this time no distraction should be allowed closer than ten feet from your dog, both during the training session and during the following break.

You should begin training by gripping the end of the line tightly. As your dog breaks and runs toward the distraction, you should silently turn ·and run in the opposite direction. There will be a powerful impact as your dog reaches the end of the line, which will be made even more forceful by your running. The impact should lift your dog into the air and hurl him backward about six feet toward you. Your dog may stand motionless, watching you, after this first correction. If he does, you should still ignore him and continue your walking routine, being always watchful for

CORRECTION
ON LONG LINE

IGNORING
THE
DISTRACTION

another charge toward the distraction. (The distraction should remain present during the entire training session, but remove it on the break.)

Let us assume that your dog does not learn on the first correction but makes a second lunge at the distraction. He may make this second try immediately after the first, or he may let time elapse before trying again. In either case, your reaction should be the same. You should silently make a turnabout, while tightly clutching the end loop of the line to your chest, and forcefully run in the opposite direction, away from your dog. After the impact you should take about four steps toward your dog, creating a slack in the line that is necessary for a further correction should he make another attempt. If more attempts are made, your silent reaction will remain the same. You should continue to correct your dog until the desired result is achieved—that result being that your dog watches *you* instead of the distraction at hand. It does not matter if your dog is barking, whining, or otherwise making any kind of oral protest. Any of this is permissible as long as he is watching you and not charging the distraction. Ignore any oral protestation your dog makes. Only correct him for *running* toward the distraction.

One of the authors is the owner of a dog-training company that trains hundreds of dogs each year. He can verify that 95 percent of all dogs trained by him learn to ignore the distraction after only one or two of these corrections. Of the remaining 5 percent some 4 percent respond after three or four corrections.

In case your conscience is bothering you about the severity of these corrections, or in case you have a couple of so-called "experts" advising you that this is no way to treat a dog, remember that there is a very important reason for the severity of the corrections. You are teaching your dog that he must not run away from you, after cats or dogs or any other distractions. This conditioning will be his life insurance policy. If he chases a cat across the street into traffic, he will be killed. Your corrections are much kinder than that. If you fail to correct hard now, some day a car or truck will do the job for you, and it will not be the least bit gentle. The author has never seen or heard of one dog, of the hundreds of dogs he trains each year, being hurt in any way by this method of correction.

By the end of the first 15-minute training session on this fifth day, your dog should be walking along fairly close to you, looking around but ignoring the distraction that took complete command of his attention in the beginning of the lesson.

This session will be followed by the usual five-minute break after the distraction has been removed by your helper. The break will be on the same 20-foot line that was just used in the training session.

After the break we will start the second session, as an exact repetition of the first. The distraction is brought in again. Most dogs will ignore it, but should your dog charge, make sure you react with an equal charge of your own. This, followed by a final five-minute break with the distraction removed, will end the fifth day's training session for the normal-average dog. Leave your dog alone for about 15 minutes, giving him a chance to think over what has just happened to him. If you did your part well, he should have a lot to think about.

The Overfriendly Dog,

The High-strung Dog—These two dogs will provide plenty of action for you with repeated lunges at distractions. They may bark a lot and should be ignored completely; they are not easily discouraged from their favorite pursuits. Once again, you cannot allow their boundless energy and enthusiasm to defeat you. Your determination and calm persistence will eventually override the dog's most insistent attempts to disregard you. If you feel at odds with the world or short-tempered, do not allow this feeling to influence your behavior with the dog. He will sense it and use your weakness to his advantage. Each time he lunges for the distraction, silently clasp your hands to your chest with a firm grip on the line, and *run* in the opposite direction. After the impact, put slack in the line by taking a few steps toward your dog. When he finally decides not to try any more charges toward the distraction, you can just turn and walk away toward the other stopping point. Walk back again toward the distraction, and if your dog tries to run to the distraction, simply repeat the process once more. After a while your dog will choose to watch you rather than the distraction. The same training format should apply, consisting of two sessions in distractions followed by the usual two five-minute breaks. This will end the fifth day's lesson.

The Aloof Dog,

The Shy-afraid Dog—These two types may only take one or two steps toward the distraction. It may take a while for them to build up their confidence to charge for a distraction. Some of them may not. Whatever your dog's choice, continue to avail him of every opportunity to pursue the distractions and receive the attendant correction. Give him the usual two sessions, followed by the two five-minute breaks. You may have to increase the distractions for these dogs. It is reasonable to increase them to maximum in this situation by having a neighbor call and coax your dog over to him, but it would be unfair to have a member of your own immediate family call him directly.

These dogs will appear to have learned with very few corrections, possibly even only one. They often will test you much later, although perhaps only the next day. Though it appears over, do not be fooled. More resistance can often crop up later on.

The Fear-biter,
The Aggressive Dog—These dogs will run directly for the distraction, giving you plenty of action, but they should respond quickly to very few corrections. It is possible that, after one of these corrections, the fear-biter or the aggressive dog may turn on you and try to bite you. With both of these dogs, *immediately after the correction give them verbal praise,* and continue walking away as before. The praise will serve to turn aside any immediate thoughts your dog may have of biting you. A few split seconds of reassurance could make the difference between a mistake on his part and a victory for you. Even if your dog comes at you growling, you must carry through your bluff. Nothing short of an all-out biting attack should deter you. The fact that he was upset enough almost to bite you indicates that he will be too upset to invite many more of these disturbing corrections. The usual walking back and forth, with the five-minute breaks, will end this routine.

THE SIXTH DAY

The Normal-average Dog—On the sixth day we will again use distractions. They should be the most extreme distractions available around your home, but bear in mind that, although most distractions are fair and should be ignored by your dog, there are some few distractions that are unfair to expect your dog to ignore at this level of his training. An example of an unfair tactic would be if the cat or dog being used as a distraction could make physical contact with your dog; or if a member of your immediate family were to call your dog by name to come to him. At this stage of your dog's training it would not be fair to expect him to ignore such distractions. On the other hand, examples of fair distractions that your dog must ignore are a neighbor or someone not in the immediate family calling your dog by name, to come to him; or a member of the immediate family yelling, jumping, clapping, running, or otherwise calling attention to himself, so long as he doesn't directly call the dog to him.

When using distractions on your dog, use fair distractions for the present. As we near the end of the course of training, your dog should listen to you against any distraction, be it fair or unfair.

You should start the sixth day's training with multiple distractions readied in your area. Once again, start walking from point to point. You can have cats and dogs staked out in different areas of your yard. Have children and adults running and calling your dog. People could be whistling or banging pots and pans. Whistling and snapping fingers is a fair distraction no matter who does it, but whistling and snapping fingers must never be used by you to call your dog to you.

This day's session will once again consist of the usual two 15-minute work sessions in distractions and the usual five-minute break after each without the distractions. This could mean walking your dog to the front of the house if distractions have been staked out in the backyard. While on the break, if your dog should go for one of the distractions you have set up, or for a real distraction that comes along unexpectedly, you should respond by implementing the usual severe correction. Make an abrupt turnabout and run forcefully the other way before you run out of line. Remember, you need a certain amount of slack in the line to effect the desired correction.

Your actions will make the critical difference between real obedience that works anywhere and anytime and the fake obedience that only works in certain situations. Your dog is learning by being corrected while on his break that he must *always* ignore distractions, with or without your direct attention. It is never afterhours for your pet. This attitude should make all subsequent training commands extremely effective and reliable.

The Overfriendly Dog,

The High-strung Dog—These dogs should be handled in the same way as the normal-average, and should be responding excellently. They should be calmed to a great degree by what you have done.

The Aloof Dog—The aloof dog still may not be walking freely by himself. You may have to drag him, and drag him you should. He may have decided that he does not like the training and, by refusing to walk, thinks he can put a halt to the training. You must make doubly sure that he is not successful in his attempt to stop you. Not only is it correct for you to walk and drag him, it is even better if you can run and drag him. He will eventually give in and walk. He is pulling a bluff and hoping that you will weaken and give up before he does. If he is successful now, then he has defeated you and successfully halted your training, proving that he is the master. However, if you persist and win out, you begin a permanent, positive change in his attitude that will insure your success with the rest of the training. Under no circumstances should the aloof dog be *coaxed* into walking. He should be dragged as you walk or run silently. The aloof dog must be made to walk because *he has to*, not because someone is coaxing him.

The Shy-afraid Dog— should be treated as the normal-average, with the exception that he *will* be verbally praised, GOOD BOY, every time he requires a correction. When he overcomes his fear of walking with you he can be praised just for walking. Take note that the shy-afraid dog is trained with almost a completely opposite technique to the aloof dog, showing, once again, the absolute necessity to categorize your dog correctly from the beginning.

The Fear-biter—On this sixth day the fear-biter is treated exactly as the normal-average dog. He is completely ignored as you walk.

The Agressive Dog—is treated exactly as the normal-average, with the exception that he should be verbally praised promptly immediately following any necessary corrections. Give him the usual two sessions and two subsequent breaks.

THE SEVENTH DAY

The Normal-average Dog,
The Overfriendly Dog,
The High-strung Dog,
The Aloof Dog,
The Shy-afraid Dog,
The Fear-biter,
The Agressive Dog—All these dogs are worked identically, in same fashion as was the normal-average dog on the sixth day. There should be no verbal communication and no coaxing or praising. This will bring all the different types of dogs as close to normal-average response as is possible, by conditioning for one entire day with no special concessions as were previously needed for any specific type of dog. You now should have a dog who walks when you walk, stops when you stop, stays reasonably close to you and watches you no matter what the distraction, and this without your giving any commands or communication whatever. The seventh day consists of the same two 15-minute sessions, followed by the

usual five-minute breaks. This ends the lesson for the seventh day.

THE EIGHTH DAY

The Normal-average Dog,
The Overfriendly Dog,
The High-strung Dog,
The Aloof Dog,
The Shy-afraid Dog,
The Fear-biter,
The Aggressive Dog—The eighth day of training consists of a test for your dog; you must plan carefully so that everything is done exactly right for the test. Remove all distractions from your training area. Have your helper ready to assist you by holding your dog's favorite distractions. This could be holding a cat in his arms, or a dog on a leash, a broom, or two pot covers clanged together, etc. You should enter the training area with your dog on the 20-foot line and begin walking across the area toward the opposite side. As you get halfway across the area, your helper should pop out from a predetermined hiding place, holding, or bringing with him, the distraction. He should move out into your clear view, with the distraction, and remain there. After the distraction is visible for three seconds; you should silently turn and walk rapidly away from it. If your dog comes with you before the line tightens to jerk or pull him, then he

COMING AROUND, IGNORING THE DISTRACTION

has passed the test. If your dog hesitates and requires a tug before he comes away with you, then he needs further testing. If your dog walks or lunges toward the distraction, he has definitely failed the test and should be corrected in the usual manner by your turning and running away in the opposite direction.

If your dog has failed the test, making a correction necessary, then you must continue for another two days with heavy distractions before you can again attempt to test your dog. If your dog stands looking at the distraction, but does not charge it, then you almost have his complete attention. Work him for another five minutes with no distraction, and then have your helper reappear abruptly with the distraction. If your dog comes around with you, he has passed the test. If he still shows interest in the distraction, work him for another two days in heavy distraction, and then test him once more. For those dogs who pass the test the first time, no further work is needed. Whether your dog passes the test the first time, or you have to go back to heavy distraction for two more days or however long it takes, he must pass the test before you can go on. Once your dog successfully passes the test you are to be congratulated, for you have done something that even some professional dog trainers are not capable of doing, or don't know how to do. You now have your dog's complete attention. Now we can begin heeling on the leash.

HEELING

THE FIRST DAY

The Normal-average Dog—This training lesson will again consist of two 15-minute work sessions followed by the usual five-minute breaks. The training area should be the same as used for the attention-getter. You should again be using your 20-foot clothesline for the breaks; it should be lying on the ground in your working area so that it can be quickly and easily installed for the breaks.

You should enter the area with your dog on the six-foot leash. Your right-hand thumb should be placed through the end loop of the leash and your hand closed upon it. With your left hand, grab the middle of the leash and again place this middle part over your right thumb. Open and close your right hand, grabbing the entire leash. Now, your left hand grabs the entire leash just below and touching your right hand. As you lift up your hands and look at them in front of you, they should be in the same basic position as if you were holding a baseball bat. Remember, both hands must be together and touching each other. Study the accompany-

PERFECT HEEL POSITION

TAKING UP THE LEASH

ing photos, so that you can grip the leash correctly.

The grip can be practiced without your dog. It just takes snapping the leash onto a fence or banister to enable you to practice till you are confident and can assume the proper grip quickly. This preparation is very important, so that you do not fumble in front of your dog and allow him to think you are not confident and in complete control.

Up to this point, we have allowed your dog to walk on either side of you. We now need him on the left side only. This is accomplished by grabbing the leash with both hands, in the proper way, and rotating your body clockwise, until your dog winds up on your left side. From now on, no matter where your dog's position, anytime you wish to begin heeling him you should spin your body in a clockwise circle that will cause your dog to wind up on your left. Once he is on your left side, you are immediately ready to begin heeling.

The heeling command consists of two words spoken in a normal, level tone of voice. It should not sound as if you are begging, nor should it sound loud and frightening. The first word is your dog's name, immediately followed by the command word HEEL. It would sound like this: Joe, HEEL. As the command is spoken, you must simultaneously begin walking, taking off on your left foot. Never give the HEEL command standing motionless expecting your dog to walk. He won't. Just give the command, Joe, HEEL, and begin walking across your training area.

The preliminary work on the long clothesline should eliminate any mad charges by your dog. But, as you walk across the training area, you will probably find your dog leading slightly out in front of you. Your reaction to his pulling or wandering out in front of you should be a quick, silent, surprise right-about turn, with a simultaneous backward jerk on the leash, as you turn and walk rapidly in the opposite direction. The next time that your dog gets out in front of you, you should again catch him with the same silent, shocking, surprise right-about turn, This turn should be used as the correction for your dog every time he gets out in front of you.

The right-about turn should be made in one quick, sharp movement and not in a slow circle. The surprise and shock of a complete 180-degree turnabout correction delivered every time he gets out in front of you, and the lack of it when he stays back by your side, will soon convince your dog that it is much more comfortable to be by your side—more comfortable than out in front of you where he can't watch you and where you may be able to catch him with your sneaky right-about turns. After a few of these hard right-about-turn corrections, you may find your dog overreacting

COMING AROUND WITH YOU

PRAISE FOR HEELING

CLOSE RIGHT-ABOUT TURN

slightly by hanging back, so that you are pulling him along. This is perfectly normal, and even good. It shows you that he is trying his best. He doesn't like the corrections and has decided to stay back where he can watch you safely. Your response to this should be not coaxing but running. You should break into a run for ten or 15 steps every time your dog starts lagging. If your dog crosses in front of you, you should again utilize the right-about-turn correction as he starts to go out in front. If he lags and crosses over in back of you, your correction should be running. If you are holding the leash in the correct manner, there will not be very much slack to allow your dog to maneuver very far out in front of you or behind you.

It is important to correct him as he starts lagging, pulling out in front, or doing anything other than heeling at your side. It will be easier for him to learn what he should be doing if he is corrected while making the mistake rather than after the fact. A great means of building your dog's confidence is praising him. The opportunity for praise occurs when you stop. Your dog should stop by your side, still standing, paying attention to you. You should praise him by stroking his head and telling him, GOOD BOY, VERY GOOD. It should be mentioned that some dogs will naturally sit upon stopping, even before having been taught the formal sit command. This, too, is perfectly fine, and your dog gets praised for whatever he does naturally, be it sit or stand. At this stage, your dog is being praised for stopping at your side when you stop, not for doing an automatic sit, which will come later on in training. Some dogs will joyfully show their anticipation of this praise by wagging their tails just before being praised. This is a very good sign. You should be walking back and forth, making right-about turns and running, where necessary, to correct lagging. Intermittently stop and praise your dog as described above. He may dislike the training, but he will love the praise. Pat him on the head rather than scratching his chest or rubbing his belly—you want to show him that his actions please you, not that you are playing a game with him.

After 15 minutes of this exercise you should walk near the area where you have laid down the long clothesline. With one smooth motion quickly attach the bolt snap of the clothesline to his collar. Still holding his leash in your hand, reach down, unhook the leash, and toss it on the ground about four feet in front of your dog, telling him in a level but cheerful voice, OKAY, THAT'S ALL. Any attempt at mad charges by your dog, after receiving this release, should be met by the usual clothesline corrections, with you running the opposite way. Your dog should, after his previous conditioning, take his break with the clothesline dragging, staying relatively close to you and keeping a watchful eye on you.

After the usual five-minute break, reinstall the leash. Take off the line and let it lay on the ground. Continue with an exact repetition of the first 15-minute session, correcting your dog for running out in front of you and for lagging. This should again be followed by a break, in the same maner as before, and that will end the first day's training session for the normal-average dog.

The Overfriendly Dog,

The High-strung Dog—These dogs are wilder than most, and may try to take advantage of you and the change in equipment by leading out in front. They should be corrected in the same basic way, with a right-about turn, with the exception that the correction must be made more intensely. Begin heeling with your dog by holding the leash as described previously. Release the lower grip you have with your right hand. (The technique that follows should be practiced without your dog on the leash, until you become proficient at it.) Holding the leash with your right hand only, as your dog runs out in front of you, open your right hand and release the body of the leash, but keep your right-hand thumb through the end loop. Close your fist around the entire end loop, holding it very securely, thereby bracing for a very severe correction. As the slack is being released, make a quick right-about turn and begin walking rapidly in the opposite direction. In this way, the impact of the right-about-turn correction is intensified by the time provided while you and your dog are moving away from each other rapidly, before the slack is taken up, causing a terrific impact. These sneaky, silent turns should be made as long as your dog continues to go out in front of you. Your left hand will not be needed at all in this routine and should only be used, after the correction, to reload the slack back into your right hand.

In all other ways, these dogs should be treated as the normal-average, including running whenever he tends to lag. As the severity of his charge diminishes, he should be treated exactly as the normal-average dog, which includes the two-handed grip on the leash as the right-about turns are made in the normal way.

The reason that the right-about turn is made without yelling NO, and without any communication between you and your dog, is simple and basic. We are trying, by our actions, to gain the attention of the dog.

117

ABOUT-TURN CORRECTION

LETTING OUT THE LEASH

RIGHT-ABOUT TURN

If we tell him NO, or communicate with or warn him in any other way that we are about to make a right-about turn, then the surprise and effectiveness of the correction is lost. To your dog, the most unpleasant aspect of the correction is the surprise, rather than the discomfort produced by the correction. If your dog does not know when you are going to make your about-turn correction, and if you don't cue him by telling him NO, then your dog is forced to *watch you*, which is exactly what we want. Another reason for making the about-turn with a silent correction is that we want the dog to think that *he* and his lack of attention caused the correction, and not that we decided to jerk him all of a sudden. Dogs that are trained with this silent method of corrections stand out and behave superior to other dogs that are trained by both vocal and physical corrections. This is true even when the latter group of dogs are trained, or even owned, by professional trainers. These dogs may behave obediently but do not keep a watchful eye on their masters, and so cannot work off leash very well.

Both categories of dogs should be praised *verbally only*. The praise should be a quick GOOD BOY, and then right off to a new HEEL command. This is done to discourage the dog from misconstruing your praise as a release from training. Work your right-about turns and stops abruptly, every couple of yards. As you stop, with your dog standing, praise him verbally, GOOD BOY, then quickly Joe, HEEL and off for another couple of yards. Stop again and repeat the praise. Two 15-minute sessions of heeling and praising, plus the five-minute breaks on the long line, will end the lesson for the first day.

The Aloof Dog—will not try running out in front of you with much force and should be handled with the two-handed leash grip. He will need much more of your running and dragging him than he will need your 'right-about-turn corrections. This is one of the few classifications of dogs that may be considered stubborn. It could take days of dragging to get him to walk freely by your side; in some rare instances it could take weeks. You must be more persistent than your dog and outlast him. You must be the final winner. Never let this dog get you angry with his refusal to walk. Just continue breaking into runs and show him he will be much more comfortable staying up and walking by your side. You must only break into a run when he is holding back, never when he is at your side. He will eventually come to believe that his lagging is the very thing that causes your running and the accompanying dragging correction. He will finally decide that the safest place to be is at your side. But let him make this decision by himself; don't try to nag or coax him into it as others would have you do.

The aloof dog should be praised just as the normal-average dog on the stops. This should be both physical and verbal praise as you stop walking and your dog remains standing. Continue your heeling routine for two 15-minute sessions, running where necessary to correct his hanging back, and making your definitive stops, praising him immediately as you stop. The aloof dog may try to sit, pulling back as you stop. Keep the leash very short so he won't be able to do this. Continue to grip the leash, providing tension and discomfort so long as he continues pulling back on the leash. Under no circumstances should you walk back to where your dog indicates his preferred position to be, and praise him there. You are undoing your victories on the heeling by allowing him to win on the stops. Move right on to a new HEEL command, and continue the routine of heeling with intermittent stops for the two 15-minute sessions and the controlled five-minute break on the long line after each.

The Shy-afraid Dog—should respond very well and very quickly to the right-about-turn corrections as used with the normal-average dog. (This means both hands are holding the leash in the normal way.) He may, after only one or two corrections, be hanging back to avoid any more corrections. Such hanging back should be dealt with in the usual manner by running. This dog should be treated in the same manner as the normal-average dog, with the exception that he should be praised verbally for walking at your side.

The shy-afraid dog should be heavily praised both verbally and physically, to build up his confidence. This should be done as soon as possible after stopping, to avoid increased fear and apprehension on his part. The shy-afraid dog may try to sit, or even lie, down, from fear. If he sits, this is okay. Just praise him and then go on to a new HEEL command. However, if he succeeds in lying down, lift him up into the sit position by putting your left hand inside his collar, on top. Lift him straight up into the sit position while praising him, thereby somewhat relaxing his apprehension. The best approach is to avoid letting your dog lie down. This can be accomplished by praising immediately upon stopping, not giving the dog a chance to lie down, and immediately moving on to a new HEEL command. The key to preventing your shy dog from lying down is immediate praise, followed by an immediate new HEEL command. Should your dog begin to lie down in spite of your praising, give an instantaneous new HEEL command and begin to walk, making it impossible for him to lie down. Work your dog on heeling for two 15-minute sessions, followed by the two five-minute breaks on the long line.

The Fear-biter-(A—that could not be worked on the previous attention-getter)-This dog would have bitten you if worked on the long clothesline. Since he has proven he will bite, certain safety precautions should be taken. The necessary equipment consists of a sturdy metal or wooden stake and 12 feet of clothesline with a bolt snap on one end. The best kind of stake is the one resembling a corkscrew that is sold in pet shops and used to tie up a dog outdoors. You will also need another chain collar, which should be bigger, stronger, and heavier than your dog's regular collar. In the center of your training area install the stake, making sure it is very securely embedded. Attach one end of the 12-foot clothesline to the stake, and to the other end attach the bolt snap with the heavy chain collar. Leave the collar laid out on the ground, already hooked to the line, and ready to be slipped over your dog's head. Bring your dog into the area on a leash. Walk directly to the collar and slip it over his head; it doesn't matter if the collar is put on frontwards or backwards. Gripping

HANGING THE AGGRESSIVE DOG

WORKING
AGGRESSIVE DOG
ON SAFETY LNE

the leash in the proper way, as described for the normal-average dog, begin walking in a counterclockwise circle around the stake, with your dog at your left side. There can be no right-about turns so long as your dog is hooked to this safety clothesline, but your dog also cannot bite you. For, if he tried, you have only to step back out of the 12-foot circle and he will be stopped cold by the 12-foot safety line.

If your dog decides he does not like this routine of walking with you and decides, in fact, to try and bite you, correct him in the following manner: while still holding the leash with both hands, as previously described, jerk in an upward direction with all your might and lift your dog into the air. Use the line as a counterforce to help keep him away from you as you lift him. At the same time scream NO to your dog, at the top of your lungs. If your dog is too big and too heavy for you to suspend in the air in this manner then put as much pressure as you can on him, even if you cannot lift him off the ground, and bellow your loud NO at him while doing this. The choking pressure should be applied until your dog halts his aggression.

This will usually take about five seconds. He should then be put down and an immediate HEEL command given, as you continue walking in your counterclockwise circle with your dog inside the circle on your left. Any further attempts to bite you will be corrected in the same way, by mid-air suspension, followed by an immediate new HEEL command. As you walk around the circle, try to position your dog so that he is fairly close to the end of the safety line but not so close that he feels a constant tug on it. Let the line be dragging on the ground so that he forgets about it.

Your dog is learning that he cannot successfully bite you and that he is better off walking with you and not trying. The first day's training will consist of one ten-minute session, and end with you removing the leash and leaving the dog tied to the stake to think over what has happened, with you remaining in the area. After the break reinstall the leash and take the dog out of the training area. This will end the first day's lesson in heeling.

The fear biter should receive verbal praise only on all the stops; keep your hands firmly gripping the leash, ready to halt any aggression should he attempt it. There are no right-about turns as yet, so just continue heeling in a counterclockwise direction, stopping every few yards to verbally praise your dog, GOOD BOY. Repeat this for the entire ten-minute session. Your dog should receive his five-minute break on the safety line as described above; then end the training session for this first day of heeling.

123

The Fear-biter-(B—who was worked on the attention-getter)-This dog should be treated exactly as the normal-average dog (two-handed leash grip), with the exception that he should be verbally praised immediately after every right-about-turn correction. This immediate praise-after-corrections helps to thwart any thoughts he may have of biting you. He should also be praised, only verbally, on your stops that will occur every couple of yards. This dog should not be corrected for lagging by running, as was the normal-average dog. Just quicken your pace slightly and keep him close to you. Two 15-minute sessions, each followed by a five-minute break on the long line, will end the first day's session on heeling for this dog.

The Aggressive Dog—Even though your dog is aggressive, it was possible for you to work him on the long line and give him fairly drastic corrections. Therefore it should be possible to work him on the leash. He also should be worked like the normal-average dog (two-handed leash grip) with the exception that he too should be verbally praised immediately following all right-about-turn corrections. If the aggressive dog should choose to hang back, you should not break into a run but should only quicken your pace, at the same time giving a new HEEL command. If the aggressive dog attempts to bite you at this stage of the training, give him two or three days' work around the circular stake and safety line, as described previously for the fear-biter, and then try again.

The safety-line work can give the fear-biter and the aggressive dog the confidence and security that will calm them and thus enable you to work them. This very often can save the dog's life, in cases where the dog would have had to be destroyed or given away because of his aggressiveness or biting problem. Some dogs may require three or four days on the safety line before they can be worked on the regular heeling routine with right-about turns. Remember, it doesn't matter how long it takes; it matters who wins, you or your dog. In most cases, with an aggressive dog, if he wins he dies, and, if you win, he can be reclaimed and live. So you must persist until you win, for both of your sakes.

Work your dog on right-abouts, keeping him close to you and verbally praising, GOOD BOY, after each correction. Stop every couple of yards and praise your dog for stopping; only verbal praise should be used. Keep a firm two-handed leash grip at all times. Work the usual two 15-minute sessions and follow with the usual two five-minute breaks on the long line. This ends the first day's heeling for the aggressive dog.

THE SECOND DAY

The Normal-average Dog—Continue with an exact repetition of the first day's training. Your dog's attention should be growing. The workout should consist of the usual two 15-minute sessions, followed by the controlled five-minute breaks after each.

The Overfriendly Dog,
The High-strung Dog—These dogs will repeat the regimen of the first day, with the absence of verbal communication on the corrections. The two 15-minute sessions, followed by the two five-minute breaks, will end the session for this second day.

The Aloof Dog,
The Shy-afraid Dog,
The Fear-biter-(A & B),
The Aggressive Dog—Each of these dogs should be drilled exactly as he was on the first day of training.

THE THIRD DAY

The Normal-average Dog—On the third day of training introduce a distraction. It should be posted at one end of the training area, and can be the usual dog or cat or other distraction as used in the attention-getter. Enter the training area from the opposite end, with your dog on leash, and give the HEEL command. You will be as far away as possible from the distraction, allowing your dog plenty of time to see it. Walk toward the distraction until you are some ten feet from it. At this point make a hard, sharp, right-about turn and your dog should come around with you. This right-about turn should be made with both hands on the leash in the usual way. If your dog comes around freely on the turn, there should be no accompanying jerk on the leash. If, however, your dog is more occupied with the distraction than with you, your right-about turn should be made with a hard jerk on the leash. Whether or not your dog needs the correction, turn and walk away from the distraction, and then do another right-about turn and walk toward the distraction again. In the middle of your area you should abruptly stop walking. Your dog should stop and stand, looking at you. At this time you should praise him physically and verbally. Then give a new HEEL command, and take off on your left foot, moving toward the distraction again. Continue walking your dog in the same way, forward and back in a straight line, alternating between about-turns and complete stops, with you praising him. Two sessions of this routine, plus the usual break after each, will end this day's training session for the normal-average dog. The breaks should be made with the distraction removed.

The Overfriendly Dog,
The High-strung Dog,
The Aloof Dog,
The Shy-afraid Dog,
The Fear-biter-(B)—These dogs should be worked exactly as the normal-average dog on this third day, with a distraction at one end of the area.

The Fear-biter-(A),
The Agggressive Dog—The fear-biter was worked on the safety line and stake for the first two days. On this third day, he should come off the stake, and both he and the aggressive dog should be worked in the same way. They should not be introduced to any distractions yet. You should heel them, making about-turns with a two-handed leash grip. Make your corrections light on the right-abouts, and give verbal praise (GOOD BOY) *as* you make the turns. Stop and praise your dog, verbally only, then give a new HEEL command and begin walking with your left foot. If these dogs start to lag, quicken your pace slightly but do not break into a run or you may encourage their aggression. The important points to remember when dealing with these two dogs are to hold the leash close, make light corrections, and to praise at the same time to discourage thoughts of biting. Do not run and do not praise with your hands. The first two days have conditioned these dogs to have considerably more respect for you and to be convinced that you are in control of the situation. You must be careful to keep them thinking this way. Their confidence in you is growing.

Proceed with heeling and right-about turns, stopping every few yards, and continue this routine for one ten-minute session before giving a five-minute break. The break should be given on the auxiliary safety line that was used for the first two days' training and still is staked out. Heel your dog to the long line to which a bolt snap is securely attached. The extra safety collar can be dispensed with now. Just snap on the long line and remove the leash, throwing it out of the circle onto the ground where your dog can see it but not reach it. Remain in the area, so your dog can see you and touch you if he wants, but not so far in that you would have difficulty removing yourself from his presence should it be necessary. Make sure the area is as distraction-free as possible. After the five-minute break, reinstall the leash, unsnap the line, and heel your dog out of the training area. This ends the third day's training session.

THE FOURTH DAY

The Normal-average Dog—should be worked as he was on the third day, with the distractions provided at one end of the training area. On this fourth day, instead of removing the distractions on the break, they should remain in the area throughout the break, but take the break at the opposite end of the area from where the distractions are. Should your dog attempt to make contact with the distractions on this break, you should implement the usual severe right-about turn, grasping the clothesline to your chest, thereby correcting the dog. In addition, any time your dog wanders off more than 12 or 15 feet from you, whether or not it is toward the distraction, he gets a correction. This straying indicates that he is more interested in investigating new things than in watching you. The correction consists of your running two or three feet in the opposite direction from where the dog is heading, then ignoring him. Repeat this as often as necessary. Remain in the area, saying nothing to your dog and ignoring him completely until you commence to work him for the second 15-minute session. Follow this by another break as outlined above, and then end the session for the fourth day.

The Overfriendly Dog,
The High-strung Dog,
The Shy-afraid Dog,
The Fear-biter-(B —that was worked on the attention-getter)-All these dogs should be worked as the normal-average dog for this fourth day. This includes the continuing distraction at one end of the training area—the distraction remaining on the breaks, which should be taken at the opposite end of the training area. All corrections are exactly as for the normal-average dog, which means using the two-handed leash grip.

The Fear-biter -(A—not worked on the attention-getter),
The Aggressive Dog—These dogs should be worked on the third day, with no distractions. The right-about turns should be made as hard as necessary, still with the two-handed leash grip. The dog has been built up sufficiently within the past three days to be able to tolerate a normal

127

training session today. This consists of two 15-minute sessions, each followed by a five-minute break. This time the breaks should be given on the long line, laid out on the ground ready to grab for about-turn corrections should your dog stray more than 12 to 15 feet from you or charge a distraction. The stake should not be used on the breaks any more. Continue to praise your dog verbally only, and this praise should occur every time you stop and every time you correct. Continue to say GOOD BOY after you correct on your right-abouts with the two-handed leash grip. Everything else remains the same.

THE FIFTH DAY

The Normal-average Dog,
The Overfriendly Dog,
The High-strung Dog,
The Aloof Dog—On this fifth day we are going to introduce some new maneuvers into the established routine. The variations will consist of new directional turns. So far we've been using only two basic maneuvers: right-about turns and stopping and praising. The right-about turns were 180 degrees, which sent you back in the opposite direction from where you were originally headed. The new turns will consist of 90-degree right- and left-angle turns.

The first turn will be the left-angle turn. It must be understood that these turns must be carried out as clean, crisp, square turns. It will not do to walk in circles or rounded corners. Your dog's attention can best be focused and brought to maximum efficiency by your catching him by surprise with quick, square turns. If your turns are not decisive, the dog's attention can wander as he begins to relax in accordance with your laxity of movement. Another good reason for quick, square turns, is that they make a much more effective correction. So, to keep your dog's attention at optimum peak and to provide the most effective corrections, make square turns. This cannot be overemphasized.

Begin the fifth day by entering your training area as usual with your dog, and proceed to work him as before. The about-turns you have made thus far have kept your dog back so that he won't try to run out in front of you. You might even have found it necessary to run, to keep your dog from lagging as a result of the overeffectiveness of the right-about-turn corrections. At this stage of his training he should be heeling at your side, but is probably walking consistently about a head out in front of you. The right-about turn has positioned your dog so he is effectively heeling with you, even though he be slightly out in front. More right-abouts will not

HEELING OUT IN FRONT

SHARP LEFT-ANGLE TURN
MADE INTO DOG

129

help to position the dog that extra ten inches or so back that becomes the true, accurate heel posture. To correct this discrepancy in positioning we shall call upon the left turn. While heeling your dog, with him once again leading you about five to ten inches, suddenly make a left turn, pivoting on your left foot, allowing your right knee to tap the dog in the face. All left turns will be made into the dog. They will be made sharply, abruptly, and without any communication or forewarning from you. After the turn, go back into the usual routine of right-about turns, stops, etc.

The other new maneuver will be a right-angle turn. This is accomplished by pivoting on the left foot and stepping out to the right, quickly, sharply, and without communication. The right-angle turn is used to correct the dog when he is heeling wide (which means walking at your side but too far out to your left). Each turn is used as a specific correction, as the right-about turn was used to correct pulling and lunging out in front of you. Every time your dog is heeling wide, use the right-angle turn as a correction. Any time you find your dog heeling slightly ahead of you, the left-angle turn should be used to correct this. The careful and consistent use of these two turns, in addition to the right-abouts, should bring your dog into perfect heel position. Practice this routine, incorporating right- and left-angle turns as needed, working your dog for two 15-minute sessions followed by two five-minute breaks, all with no distractions.

The Shy-afraid Dog,
The Fear-biter-(both),
The Aggressive Dog—All these dogs should be worked as the normal-average for the fifth day, keeping the dog close, except that the left- and right-angle turns should be made more slowly. The turns should be square, but the impact will not be as severe. These dogs should also be praised (GOOD BOY) immediately after the corrections. The training should consist of two 15-minute sessions followed by the two five-minute breaks on the long line. There are no distractions today.

THE SIXTH DAY

The Normal-average Dog,
The Overfriendly Dog,
The High-strung Dog,
The Aloof Dog,
The Shy-afraid Dog,
The Fear-biter-(both),
The Aggressive Dog—All these dogs should be worked as they were on

HEELING WIDE

HT-ANGLE-TURN CORRECTION

HEELING ALONGSIDE AGAIN

131

the fifth day of heeling. This includes right-about turns, right-angle turns, left-angle turns, and, when necessary, running to compensate for lagging. The difference for the sixth day is that you should again introduce distractions at one end of the training area. This will be the first day of distractions for the fear-biter and the aggressive dog. Leave the distractions present during the breaks and take the breaks at the end opposite to the distractions. Vary your walking pattern, making a series of left, right, and right-about turns. React appropriately, according to your dog's response to the distractions. If your dog is right with you, he should receive no corrections as you maneuver him through the turns. Work your dog for two 15-minute sessions followed by two five-minute breaks, with the distractions present on the breaks. This will end the sixth day's training session for your dog.

THE SEVENTH DAY

The Normal-average Dog,
The Overfriendly Dog,
The High-strung Dog,
The Aloof Dog,
The Shy-afraid Dog,
The Fear-biter-(both),
The Aggressive Dog— All these dogs should be worked as they were on the previous day, except that there should be multiple distractions scattered throughout the area. This could be dogs and cats, adults and children, totaling three or four varied distractions. You should heel your dog throughout this area, getting no closer than eight to ten feet to any distraction, and making any necessary corrections. Take the breaks with the distractions remaining in the area, and take the breaks about 20 feet from the nearest distraction. Two 15-minute sessions followed by the usual two five-minute breaks will end the seventh day of training.

THE EIGHTH DAY

The Normal-average Dog,
The Overfriendly Dog,
The High-strung Dog,
The Aloof Dog,
The Shy-afraid Dog,
The Fear-biter-(both),
The Aggressive Dog—For all the dogs the routine will be an exact repetition of the previous day's training.

THE NINTH DAY

The Normal-average Dog,
The Overfriendly Dog,
The High-strung Dog,
The Aloof Dog,
The Shy-afraid Dog,
The Fear-biter-(both),
The Aggressive Dog—All these dogs should now be taken into heavy distractions outside of the training area. The best place would be a shopping center. Your dog must be taken to a place where he does not normally walk, at least two blocks away from your normal work area. Three o'clock is a good time to walk your dog near a school. The children getting out will provide plentiful distractions. Work your dog for two 15-minute sessions, followed by two controlled five-minute breaks on the six-foot leash, *not the long line.* After the second five-minute break, heel or drive your dog home. He has now passed the final test of ultimate distractions, and you are to be congratulated for developing a very attentive dog. Your dog is now ready to begin the Sit.

THE SIT

The sit is a basic primary command used to control your dog. When used with heeling, it is a great way of gaining your dog's attention. When used with the stay, it can change your dog's attitude in a favorable way and can build his confidence in himself and in you.

THE FIRST DAY—

The Normal-average Dog—With no distractions in the training area, begin working your dog on all maneuvers, including right- and left-angle and right-about turns. Up to now you have been praising your dog just for stopping and standing still at your side when you stop. Today we will begin to change that routine. Holding your dog close to you, with the two-handed leash grip, you should come to a stop. As you do so, let go of the leash with your left hand and continue to hold it only with your right hand. Now give the command SIT, prefaced by your dog's name. The command will sound like this, Dream, SIT. Once again, neither bellow nor whisper to your dog; give the command in a clear, emotionless tone. Give the command only once, and immediately force your dog to sit by placing your open left hand on his rear and pushing steadily down, as you exert steady upward pressure on the leash with your right hand. This upward pressure is not a jerk on the leash, but a steady, constant, strong upward pressure that will stop the instant your dog is sitting. Once your dog is sitting, he should receive praise, just as he did in heeling when he stopped and stood at your side. Immediately after the praise you should move off with a new HEEL command: Dream, HEEL. There should be no more standing stops as before. On all future stops you should command, Dream, SIT, and immediately place him on the sit as described above. Continue the routine of heeling, right and left turns, and right-about turns, stopping every few yards. At every stop place your dog physically on sits. As soon as he sits, praise him, GOOD BOY, and proceed with a new HEEL command. Do not nag your dog with repetitions of SIT, SIT, SIT. Each command should be given *only once*, and all commands are prefaced by your dog's name, Dream, SIT; Dream, HEEL; etc. Vary your routine of turns and sit placements so as not to become predictable and allow your dog to anticipate your moves. Work him for two 15-minute sessions, followed by two five-minute breaks with no distractions. This ends the first day's session.

The Overfriendly Dog,

The High-strung Dog—These dogs should be worked just as the normal-average in placing on the sit. The only exception may be that they will not hold the sit very long. They may sit and then hop right up again. If these dogs receive an overabundance of praise you will be encouraging such actions. Many of these dogs, when praised, take that praise as their cue to take advantage of you, and they will then jump all over you wildly. If this is the case, you should reduce the amount of praise your dog receives by not praising him physically at all: give only a quick verbal GOOD BOY, and immediately move on to a new HEEL command. The best way to gauge the correct amount of praise to give your dog is to see how much advantage he takes of you when you praise him. As days go by and he becomes more steady and is able to handle more praise, he can get more. In all respects, work your dog through the same routine as for the normal-average dog, with two 15-minute sessions followed by two five-minute breaks, with no distractions.

The Aloof Dog—will be placed on the sit just as the normal-average dog. He can be given a normal amount of praise. If there is an excessive amount of resistance to being placed, you must increase the upward pressure on the leash, which must cease immediately as soon as he sits. Other than that, these dogs should be worked as the normal-average dog with

THE SIT

THE SIT PLACEMENT

the usual two 15-minute sessions, followed by two five-minute breaks with no distractions.

The Shy-afraid Dog,
The Fear-biter-(both A & B are now worked as one),
The Aggressive Dog—These dogs should be worked just as the normal-average, with the exception that, when placing them on the sit, the upward pressure with the right hand should be more gentle and the angle of the leash should be slightly to the front. In addition, these dogs should be praised, GOOD BOY, directly after the SIT command, before they are actually sitting. This will lessen their fear and make them go down easier. Once they are sitting give them a lot of praise, which should now include physical praise, as much as possible before moving on to a new HEEL command. With each new phase of learning, the dogs will react with uncertainty and fear. The best defense against this is effusive praise to diminish their insecurity. Work these dogs as usual, with the two 15-minute sessions followed by the two five-minute breaks, with no distractions.

THE SECOND DAY

The Normal-average Dog,
The Overfriendly Dog,
The High-strung Dog,
The Aloof Dog,
The Shy-afraid Dog,
The Fear-biter-(A & B),
The Aggressive Dog—Work all the dogs just as on the first day of placing on sits, with the respective special techniques appropriate to each type of dog.

THE THIRD DAY

The Normal-average Dog—can now be placed on sits with multiple distractions present throughout the area. The place you choose can be in or out of your normal work area, so long as the distractions are numerous. Work your dog in the same routine as for the first two days, making the left- and right-angle turns and right-about turns, and running where appropriate. Every few yards, stop, shorten up on the leash, say your dog's name, and then the command, SIT. Pull up and press down simultaneously, and praise your dog, GOOD BOY. Work him in this routine for the usual two 15-minute sessions, and take the two five-minute breaks on the long line except in cases where you are out of the normal work area, such as in a shopping center, etc. In this situation, the breaks should be taken on the six-foot leash. This completes the third day's session for the normal-average dog.

The Overfriendly Dog,
The High-strung Dog—Work these dogs extra firmly on the sit placements, putting very firm upward tension on the leash with your right hand and cutting the praise very short. Move on to a new HEEL command quickly. As this approach is repeated again and again, you will begin to see more positive results. The dog is learning that he cannot deter you from your objective with his fancy footwork. You must understand that your dog's seemingly friendly action of jumping on you when you praise him is really an attempt on his part to put an end to the training session. Work the full routine as described for the normal-average dog, showing him that you do not fall for this ploy. Give him the two 15-minute sessions and the two five-minute breaks on the long line. If you are working out of your area, such as in a shopping center, take the breaks on the six-foot leash.

The Aloof Dog—should be handled just as the normal-average, except that you should continue to vary the routine at such a rapid pace that you excite his interest. If you do not make constant, definitive moves, your stubborn dog will become lethargic and resume his holding back, just as he started to do at the outset of training. Place him quickly, command crisply, and praise lavishly, moving from technique to technique without any lag. In this way you will leave no time for him to think up ways to resist you. Work your dog for the usual sessions and two five-minute breaks on the long line, except if you are out of your normal work area; in that case, use the six-foot leash for the breaks.

The Shy-afraid Dog—Work this dog just as the normal-average, except that your praise, GOOD BOY, should be given *as* you are placing the dog as well as after placing him. Praise lavishly. Work two 15-minute sessions followed by two five-minute breaks on the long line. If you are out of your normal work area, take the breaks on the six-foot leash.

The Fear-biter-(A&B),
The Aggressive Dog—These dogs should be placed on sits as the normal-average dog, except that, with the larger breeds, the tension should be

straight up on the leash. Your fist should rotate toward your face, and the right forearm should bend close into your body, blocking your face and vital parts from your dog's mouth. With the smaller dogs, the leash grip should be shortened and the tension should be directed toward the front of the dog and away from you. The pressure on the rump remains the same with both size dogs. Do not forget to praise, GOOD BOY, as you are placing your dog, directly after the command as well as when he is sitting. Keep the right-hand leash tension gentle, and release it immediately as your dog sits. Your praise should continue to be physical as well as verbal, for the more you can touch your dog the more confident it will make him in you. If your dog seems nervous and starts to show aggression, return to verbal praise only. Work the dog for two 15-minute sessions with the two five-minute breaks on the long line, unless your work area is very public and difficult in which to exercise control, in which case the six-foot leash should be used for the breaks.

PLACING AGGRESSIVE DOG ON SITS, USING A FOREARM BLOCK

THE FOURTH DAY

The Normal-average Dog,
The Overfriendly Dog,
The High-strung Dog,
The Aloof Dog,
The Shy-afraid Dog,
The Fear-biter-(A & B),
The Aggressive Dog—All of the dogs should be worked just as they were on the third day of sit placement, with distractions. You should also concentrate on the heeling, to obtain maximum precision placement of your dog in the heel position. With every new technique, constant reinforcement is necessary in the familiar material to maintain peak performance and accuracy. Work your dog for the usual two 15-minute sessions, with the controlled five-minute breaks on the long line or the six-foot leash, depending upon what the situation requires.

THE FIFTH DAY

The Normal-average Dog,
The Overfriendly Dog,
The High-strung Dog,
The Aloof Dog,
The Shy-afraid Dog,
The Fear-biter-(A & B),
The Aggressive Dog—Work all the dogs just as you did on the third and fourth days of sit placement. They should again be placed on sits during multiple distractions. Continue working all the obediences, and varying the routine so that your dog does not predict your movements or commands.

If you are having any difficulty in executing square right and left turns, both of which require you to pivot on the left foot, work through the motions without the dog until your footwork is very secure. Continue to train yourself in quick counterresponses to whatever mistakes in heeling position your dog may succumb to. As these are repeated, your trigger-quick responses should become second nature to you and you can always be assured a perfect heel position from your dog. Work the dog for the two 15-minute sessions followed by the two five-minute breaks, either on the long line or on the six-foot leash, depending on the work area you have chosen.

The Normal-average Dog,
The Overfriendly Dog—With absolutely no distractions in the training area, enter the area, heeling your dog with a slightly shortened two-handed leash grip. Begin heeling your dog and, as you walk, prepare yourself mentally for your next stop. No longer will you place your dog and no longer will you tell him to sit. You should say nothing as you stop. Just remain ready, as you now come to a complete stop. If your dog sits—praise him. If your dog does not, correct him in the following manner: without saying a word, and still gripping the leash with both hands, jerk with all your might straight upward above the dog. Do not say SIT. Do not say NO. Just give one terrifically hard correction. The correction should be so hard and forceful that it actually forces your dog into the sit position.

If your dog sits at this time, praise him, GOOD BOY. If your dog is not sitting by this time, the fault is not his but yours, in that you have undercorrected him by not jerking hard enough. If this is the case, you

THE SIT CORRECTION

should now give a vocal SIT command, such as Dream, SIT. If he sits, praise him. If not, you should then correct again in a similar manner, only much harder this time, so as to force him into the sit position with your correction. If he sits after this correction, praise him, GOOD BOY. Should your dog, for some reason, still remain standing and refuse to sit, you are definitely undercorrecting him. Most dogs respond to one or two proper corrections. Your task is to win out by alternating a correction and a command for as long as is necessary to make your dog sit. This exercise must only end one way, with your dog sitting.

Do not approach the correction with the fear that you may be hurting your dog. You will not. The dog must have a correction that will be memorable to him for the rest of his life, so that he will perform reliably in ultimate distractions and in any given situation. You have ade-quately prepared him for what you expect from him, with five days of placement. Now you can justify a very forceful correction. We are not using a nagging approach to training. That would be appropriate if you were content to sound like a broken record with SIT, SIT, SIT blurted pleadingly at your dog, as his unreliability turns your face to crimson in sheer exhaustion and embarrassment. What may appear to be the hardest method is, in reality, the kindest, and causes the least amount of punishment to your dog.

Remember to correct silently, then wait a few seconds and give a new command, Dream, SIT; then wait a few seconds and give another silent, hard correction. Be careful not to say SIT as you are correcting him. Correction and command must be kept separate. The few seconds' wait between actions is to give your dog a chance to sit, thereby receiving his reward—your praise. Praise your dog whether he sits on the correc-tion or on the command. He is being praised for sitting. How he got there is incidental to the praise; finally, by whatever means is needed, your dog is sitting.

Directly after the praise, move on to a new HEEL command. Make another definitive stop and wait a second or two to give your dog a chance to react. Most dogs will sit after the initial introduction to the sit correction. Should your dog decide not to sit, promptly react with another forceful, silent sit correction. If he sits this time, praise him and move on to a new HEEL command, Dream, HEEL. If not, give a new SIT command, and keep alternating, as before, with corrections and commands until you win out. Plan your stops and make them crisp and decisive. Where you decide to stop is where your dog must sit. Re-member that, should your dog not sit upon your stop, the silent correction comes first, not the SIT command.

Work your dog in the established routine of heeling, with all turns. This time you should have an automatic sit on every stop instead of the previous sit placement. Never go back to *placing* your dog on sits now that he has received the sit correction. You no longer have to show your dog what you want; you now have only to enforce it *every time you stop*. Your dog may attempt to take advantage of you if you are involved in other things. Never tell your dog to do anything unless you are able to enforce it, and that means the leash and collar must be on for now. Resist the temptation to show off the obedience to your friends until you and the dog are firmly entrenched in each new routine and able to handle great distractions. Work your dog in the usual two 15-minute sessions, without distractions, and take the two five-minute breaks on the long line, also without distractions.

The High-strung Dog—should be worked just as the normal-average dog, with the exception that you may find him taking a few steps around in front of you and sitting there. This shows that he is trying to cooperate but is a little confused as to where he should sit. A further teaching process is needed in this case, to solve this specific problem. It should be

THE AUTOMATIC SIT

corrected now before it is repeated too many times. Anything that is repeated in dog training is learned, whether it be right or wrong. Therefore we must correct any errors in positioning before they become habits. Whether your dog is swinging his rear out and facing you, or whether he walks around a few steps in front of you and then sits facing you, both positions are wrong and must be corrected. Correct these mistakes by making all of your stops against a wall, a tree, a fence, or any such available object so as to prevent your dog from swinging his rear out sideways. The next technique should be to quicken your leash corrections for the automatic sit, so that the dog has no choice but to sit immediately at your side where he stops. Thus he is receiving the correction before he has time to take the two or three extra steps that will bring him around in front of you. Both techniques will be most effective when used together.

The Aloof Dog—should be treated just as the normal-average dog, with good hard corrections and no coaxing or pleading. This dog usually requires a few extra corrections, which must be consistently very hard to discourage further resistance. This dog has enough natural resistance built in so we don't want to encourage any more. Once the aloof dog is sitting, he may renew his reluctance to walk with you. Your response to this should be to break into short runs as before, until he is once again walking at your side and sitting when you stop. The dog's technique is to try to fool or bluff his owner into thinking that he really doesn't know what is expected of him. But if you have followed the day-by-day procedure as outlined in this book, you can rest assured that he knows exactly what you want. Your reaction to his resistance must be solid, firm, very hard corrections. You must have patience to outlast his stubbornness. Continue in the routine until you win the victory for you and your dog.

The Shy-afraid Dog—should be treated as the normal-average dog, except that there should be plenty of praise once he is sitting. He should respond very well to the sit corrections, and require very few of them. With this dog you may also encounter the sitting sideways or sitting out in front that was discussed with the high-strung dog. To counteract these tendencies, use the two methods—heeling alongside a solid object, plus very quick corrections—as outlined in detail for the high-strung dog.

With the shy-afraid dog you may encounter an overreaction to the sit correction in that he lies down. This is caused by fear. He lies down in submission. Once again, this lying down is a mistake and, if repeated, is learned. So, it must be stopped immediately. To prevent it, as you come to a stop shorten up on your leash grip and verbally praise your dog, GOOD BOY, as he starts to sit. At the same time tighten up on the leash tension, not allowing the dog to lie down, and continue praising him as he sits. The praise will help to allay the fear that is causing him to lie down, while the steady upward pressure on the leash is making it physically impossible for him to lie down. If he remains sitting, you may physically praise him with your left hand on top of his head for a few seconds before giving him a new HEEL command.

If, when you stop, your dog is still trying his best to lie down, then, immediately after a quick GOOD BOY, heel him off again: Joe, HEEL. Your praise must be fast enough to be dispensed before he starts to lie down. This quick praising and immediate moving off with a new HEEL command does not give him the time to lie down. As this is repeated you are creating an environment where he is not able to lie down but, contrarily, is repeating the correct thing and thereby building up his confidence. If your dog responds to the sit correction by refusing to walk, you should correct him by breaking into short runs at frequent intervals. With the shy-afraid dog, every new phase of training will bring a temporary setback to his confidence but, as each new command is learned and repeated, his confidence will be built back up again. This very positive approach to training the shy-afraid dog will actually build his self-confidence, where nagging, coaxing methods will produce a more frightened dog that will do his obedience poorly and unreliably at best.

The Fear-biter-(A & B),
The Aggressive Dog—Reinstall the stake and safety line as previously used in the first two days of heeling. Begin heeling your dog counter-clockwise around the stake, at the end of the safety line. Heel him around two complete circles and then make your first stop. For the first stop only, place him on a sit. This should be the last placement for these dogs. Give a HEEL command immediately and start walking once around the circle, making sure you are at the end of the safety-line tension. Now make your stop and give the verbal command, Dream, SIT. Give the command clearly and firmly, and give it only once. If your dog sits, praise him and move on with a new HEEL command. If not, correct in the following manner: exactly three seconds after giving your command, jerk straight up so forcefully that it forces your dog to sit. This correction should be done silently. If your dog now sits, you should praise him and move on with a new HEEL command. If not, remain standing where you are and repeat the command, Dream, SIT. Three seconds

144

later, you should again correct in a strong upward direction, with both hands on the leash. He should now be sitting. You should praise him and walk on with a new HEEL command.

Continue this routine of a command and a correction until your dog is sitting on command. Remember to make your corrections very, very hard. This will discourage your dog's resisting you, and minimize the corrections he will have to take. Walk on with a new HEEL command, and halfway around the circle make another stop. Again give the command, Dream, SIT, and, three seconds later, the correction if he is not sitting. Do not forget to praise your dog every time he sits, whether it be after the command or after the correction.

Once he is sitting and has been praised, give a HEEL command and walk another half-turn around the circle and stop again, giving a new command, Dream, SIT. If he sits, praise him. If not, give the correction, and continue alternating in this manner until you win out. Keep making very hard corrections, and continue to keep just within the outer perimeter of the safety line. Give him one 15-minute session of this, followed by a five-minute break on a spare long line that will be lying on the ground in the work area, with a bolt snap securely attached. Unsnap the staked line, snap on the long line, and then unsnap the leash and toss it on the ground, telling your dog, OKAY, THAT'S ALL, and letting him walk freely on the long line for his break.

AGGRESSIVE DOG BEING
HUNG ON SAFETY LINE.

For the second 15-minute session, snap on the leash, release the auxiliary long line, take your dog to the safety stake, snap on the safety line, and begin heeling in a counterclockwise circle as before. Give the HEEL command and begin walking. Complete two rotations around the circle and then stop. Wait three seconds and then, if your dog is not sitting, *saying nothing*, give a very hard physical correction as before, in an upward direction. If he sits, praise him and walk on, giving a new HEEL command. On your next stop repeat the procedure: the silent stop, and three seconds later the correction if needed. Once your dog sits, praise him and walk on. You now have accomplished the automatic sit. Your dog should be sitting by your side without a command each time you stop. After this second session of 15 minutes, give him another break with the auxiliary clothesline dragging on the ground. This will end the training session for the day.

If, while your dog is first being corrected, he attempts to bite you, you should lift quickly, straight upwards with both hands on the leash, while using the leverage of the safety line to prevent the dog from reaching you and to help control him. Bellow the single word NO!!!, as you lift and hold him up in the air. Do not put him down until he stops all aggressive action. Then repeat the command, Dream, SIT. Should he not sit, you should administer a very severe sit correction, which will be silent, and alternate command with correction until you win out. If he attempts again to bite you, again lift straight up in the air, raising your dog off the ground and bellowing another loud NO!!!. Hold him up until he halts all aggression and longs to be back on all fours again. Command him to sit again, Dream, SIT, and praise him verbally when he does so, quickly moving on to another new HEEL command.

The important thing to remember is that there are two corrections: one jerking correction for not sitting, and one lifting-and-holding-up correction for attempting to bite you. You must administer the proper correction for each mistake. Secondly, the correction for not sitting is silent, whereas the correction for attempting to bite is a very loud, verbal NO, as well as physically lifting in the air. Should you find it necessary to administer the lifting correction, it is highly important that you do not let time elapse after the correction in which you do nothing; or get sudden pangs of guilt and decide to pet your dog to assuage your conscience for the terrible thing you think you have just done to him. Immediately give a new SIT command. The SIT command is issued rather than the HEEL command, because until he has sat, even with corrections, it is not yet over. Once he is sitting, you can give quick verbal praise and move on to a new HEEL command. Rarely will you find more than two lifting corrections necessary if you have done them properly, and most often one will suffice. Continue with your training program, walking counterclockwise and administering the proper commands, as though nothing ususual has occurred. You should be getting automatic sits every time now. If you don't, you know what to do. Remember, your dog does not hear the word *sit* anymore, except if it occurs after a needed correction and he still is not sitting.

THE SEVENTH DAY

The Normal-average Dog,
The Overfriendly Dog,
The High-strung Dog,
The Aloof Dog,
The Shy-afraid Dog—Work all these dogs as they were worked on the sixth day, enforcing the automatic sit at all times. Today you should introduce a distraction at one end of the work area, and enter the area from the opposite side, continuing to work your way toward the distraction. Now you have two ways of commanding your dog's attention over a distraction; up to now you had only the right-about turns. When working in distraction, if your dog's attention starts to focus on the distraction, simply stop walking immediately and your dog should sit quickly. If he does not, an immediate sit correction should refocus his attention upon you. So now you can use both the right-about turn as well as the automatic sit to gain your dog's quick attention in a distracting situation. He is learning that a distraction is both a trap for him and the signal to become extra attentive to your movements and commands. Work your dog for the usual two 15-minute sessions, with the subsequent two five-minute breaks on the long line. The distractions should remain present on the breaks. This ends the seventh day of the sit for your dog.

The Fear-biter,
The Aggressive Dog—Bring your dog out and hook him to the stake. Start heeling him around the stake on the safety line. After two complete revolutions, make your stop. Say nothing. If your dog sits, verbally praise him. If he does not sit, correct with a hard jerk; give praise once he is sitting. Then move on with a new HEEL command. When he has made three automatic sits on consecutive stops, or has taken three consecutive corrections and then sat after them, he is ready to be worked off the safety line.

Unsnap the bolt, leaving the extra chain collar hanging loosely around his neck. It is very important that there be no distractions in your work area, as your dog can renew his resistance at an inopportune moment for you. The progress and conditioning of your fear-biter or aggressive dog must advance in very gradual stages. Skipping a stage by prematurely introducing uncontrollable or uncontrolled distractions will make enforcement much more difficult for you and could cause a completely unnecessary setback in your dog's training progress. He is convinced from the first day's corrections that you can enforce what you require of him. Be sure to keep him thinking that way. Gradually he should be so completely convinced of your capability that he won't even think about contesting your will. This will happen, but it happens slowly and in stages.

Once your dog is able to take sit corrections from you, he is able to join the other dogs and work in distractions. Work him for two 15-minute sessions, following each with a five-minute break on the long line. Your dog is now off the stake for the breaks as well as for the work sessions. There are no distractions today.

THE EIGHTH DAY

The Normal-average Dog,
The Overfriendly Dog,
The High-strung Dog,
The Aloof Dog,
The Shy-afraid Dog—All of these dogs should again work in distractions, using both the automatic sit as well as the right-about turns to keep your dog's attention upon you. Today, they should be taken to a shopping center or crowded street and worked in multiple distractions. Do not allow children or adults walking by to make contact with your dog, and don't get into any conversations with passers-by. People may be interested in what you are doing, but you will lose control over the situation if you indulge their interest. Do not be afraid to correct as hard as necessary, even though some people may whisper under their breath at your "brutality."

Work your dog for one 20-minute session with no break, and then walk or drive him home.

The Fear-biter,
The Aggressive Dog—Today these dogs should be worked off the safety line, and a distraction should be introduced at one end of the training area. You should work your dog toward and then away from the distrac-

tion, in the usual manner, employing the right-abouts and the automatic sits to command your dog's attention over the distraction. You should enter the training area opposite to the distraction, continuing to work your dog toward it. Never come closer to the distraction than ten feet. Vary your controls by stopping abruptly, thereby enforcing the automatic sit, together with right-about turns requiring your dog to come around with you. If you want more critical attention from your dog, make more frequent stops. You can walk as little as one or two steps, and still require another automatic sit. If your dog seems very interested in the distraction, your constant stops will require so much of his attention that his interest in the distraction will soon wane.

Work your dog for two 15-minute sessions, followed by two five-minute breaks on the long line. The distraction should remain present, but your breaks are taken at the opposite end of the work area from the distraction.

THE NINTH DAY

The Normal-average Dog,
The Overfriendly Dog,
The High-strung Dog,
The Aloof Dog,
The Shy-afraid Dog—All these dogs should again be worked in heavy distractions at a shopping center, etc., just as in the previous day's training. This is the ultimate in distractions, and your dog should be working well for you by this time.

Work your dog for one 20-minute session today, with no break. Your dog is now ready to begin the Stay.

The Fear-biter,
The Aggressive Dog—These dogs should now be worked in heavy distractions at a shopping center. This is a multiple-distraction situation that is the most difficult for your dog to overcome. It is vitally important that *you,* as well as your dog, ignore the distractions completely. Do not converse with curiosity seekers, or react to comments by passers-by. Above all, do not allow people to pet your dog. This situation takes every ounce of your control and attention. In order to accomplish your goals, don't allow anything to interfere with your efforts or it will diminish your results.

This ninth day of work must be repeated for two additional days in heavy distractions, making a total of 11 days on sits. Each session will be

20 minutes in duration, with no breaks. For these two categories of dogs, a total of three days in heavy distractions should prepare them sufficiently so that they should now be ready to begin the Stay.

THE SIT-STAY

THE FIRST DAY

The Normal-average Dog—On this first day of the Sit-Stay, there will be no distractions used. Enter the training area with your dog on the leash and begin your heeling routine as usual. Work your dog with the customary stops, automatic sits, and the usual turns. After two or three minutes, when your dog is thoroughly warmed up and working well, you are ready to begin the mechanics of teaching him to stay.

Begin heeling your dog. As you come to a complete stop and he is sitting by your side, let go of the leash with your left hand but continue holding it with your right. Swing your left hand across your body, with palm facing your dog and fingers open. Your hand should move slowly toward his face, stopping about three inches from his nose. This action should be accompanied by the command, Dream, STAY. All commands are prefaced by the dog's name, Dream, STAY, with the command word accentuated rather than the dog's name. You should now leave your dog by stepping out in front of him with your right foot. Then turn back, facing toward your dog, by pivoting on your right heel as you take a second step out with your left, drawing it alongside your right foot. You are now facing your dog. You should maintain the stay signal with your left hand, as you also maintain an upward tension on the leash with your right hand. After three seconds have elapsed you should immediately return to the heel position by stepping back to your dog's side with your left foot, and pivoting on your left heel clockwise as you then step back with your right foot. As soon as you have returned to the heel position, promptly release the tension on the leash and praise your dog, GOOD BOY. Move off with a new HEEL command and vary the routine, doing a couple of automatic sits.

We are now ready to try another Sit-Stay. Make another stop, let go of the leash with your left hand, and give the STAY command and hand signal as before, Dream, STAY. Repeating the same footwork as before, leave your dog, stepping out and facing him as you maintain the tension on the leash with your right hand. With the left hand, maintain the stay signal in front of his face. Return to your dog's side, as previously described, and praise him. Then begin walking with a new HEEL com-

HEELING IN DISTRACTIONS

AUTOMATIC SIT IN DISTRACTIONS

AUTOMATIC SIT WITH DISTRACTION AT ONE END

151

THE SIT-STAY

SIT-STAY COMMAND AND SIGNAL

STEPPING OUT IN FRONT WITH
RIGHT FOOT, MAINTAINING
TENSION ON LEASH

mand, Dream, HEEL. Continue working your dog on this complete routine, implementing the Sit-Stay about every third stop, or approximately every minute. Work your dog with no distractions for the usual two 15-minute sessions followed by the two five-minute breaks. This will end the first day's training on the Sit-Stay.

It is important to mention at this time that the STAY command should be given only once, and not repeated in a nagging manner. There should be no need to repeat the command, because your dog is not able to break (get up from) the stay at this time. The tension exerted on the leash with your right hand, holds the dog in place, making it impossible for him to get up. Also, the brief period of time that your dog is on the stay (two to three seconds) does not even give him enough time to think about breaking. Both of these safeguards, the upward tension and the short time, will be maintained throughout the entire first lesson.

The Overfriendly Dog,
The High-strung Dog—Both of these dogs will have more of a tendency to break the stay than any of the other dogs. The key to success with these dogs will be to make certain that they are not able to break the stay. This is done, again, with very short stays and increased upward tension on the leash, holding your dog firmly in place. If the dog overreacts to your physical praise when you return, by jumping around, dispense with physical praise and reduce the verbal to a very quick GOOD BOY, immediately followed by a new HEEL command.

The Aloof Dog—is worked just as the normal-average, with no deviation in routine.

The Shy-afraid Dog—should be worked like the normal-average dog, but with effusive praise on the return. Very short stays will make things easier for dogs in this category.

The Fear-biter,
The Aggressive Dog—should be worked as the normal-average, except that the sweep of the hand on the stay signal should be considerably curtailed. Make only a very conservative gesture, holding your hand an inch or two from your body. *Never* push your hand into the dog's face, which could be misconstrued by your dog as aggression on your part. Keep the palm open but close to your body while maintaining the signal with the left hand, and the upward tension with the right hand. When you return, give verbal praise only, and begin dispensing praise as you

OUT IN FRONT, MAINTAINING
TENSION ON LEASH

RETURNING TO HEEL

TAKE UP LEASH AND PRAISE

154

are returning rather than waiting until you are back at heel position. This should serve to dispel his apprehension. Do not run back to his side as you return, but return slowly, praising him verbally as you do so. Once you are back at heel position, move on to a new HEEL command and take your dog through his complete routine, including frequent stays (every 60 seconds approximately), for two 15-minute sessions followed by two five-minute breaks, all with no distractions.

STAY SIGNAL FOR AGGRESSIVE DOG, HAND CLOSE TO BODY

THE SECOND DAY

The Normal-average Dog—Enter the training area with your dog on leash. Begin taking him through his paces just as you did on the first day of the Sit-Stay. Begin by making stops, enforcing the automatic sit if necessary. As your dog gets into the work routine, prepare for your next stop, which will be a Sit-Stay. Leave your dog as before. Step out with the described footwork and turn facing your dog. Continue holding the stay signal while maintaining tension on the leash with your right hand. After two or three seconds return to heel position, take up the leash, and then praise your dog. Move on with a new HEEL command.

After a few more stops with just an automatic sit, again command your dog, Dream, STAY, with the proper accompanying hand signal. Move out in front of your dog, this time releasing the upward tension on the leash and also dropping your hand to your side. Count five seconds to yourself, then immediately return to your dog's side, take up the leash, and then praise him. Continue working your dog on his complete routine and prepare for another Sit-Stay. Again leave your dog, giving the command and signal, Dream, STAY. Move out in front, releasing the tension and dropping your hand to your side. Remain standing motionless and watching your dog for another five seconds. Again return to your dog's side, take up the leash, and praise him. Continue working your dog on five-second stays with released tension and your hand dropped to your side, after having given the signal. Work this way for the first 15 minutes. After this time give your dog his usual break on the long line.

After the break switch once again to the leash and begin heeling your dog across the training area. Come to a stop. Give the STAY command and signal. Leave your dog with the usual footwork. Remember to drop the hand signal once again and release the tension on the leash. When you are out in front, smoothly step back *one step* and remain standing motionless for five seconds. Return to your dog's side, take up the leash, and then praise him. Continue working the complete routine, interspersing stays at regular intervals. The second 15-minute work session differs from the first only in the respect that you should back up one step once you are out in front of your dog. The stay should still be held for five seconds, and you should always take up the leash with the proper hand grip before praising your dog. This will teach him to remain holding the Stay *after* you return to him. He must wait until you signal, by your praise, that he is released. After the second 15-minute work session, take the usual five-minute break on the long line and end the lesson for this second day of Sit-Stays for your normal-average dog.

The Overfriendly Dog,

The High-strung Dog—These dogs should be worked just as the normal-average, with the exception that you should give only verbal praise and, upon returning, hesitate an extra two or three seconds before praising. It is very important that you give the command and hand signal only once. Do not nag with repetitive commands and signals. The clearer and louder your command is given, the longer it will last in your dog's mind. It is very important, when working dogs in this category, that you do not convey to them an excited form of behavior on your part. Go through every routine with a calm, methodical approach. The excited approach would mirror your dog's behavior, and would only serve to make him

156

STAY SIGNAL   AND COMMAND

RETURN AND PRAISE   OUT IN FRONT, ONE STEP BACK

more high-strung or overexuberant. Your dog is looking for an excuse to flip out and end the work session. Don't let your mannerisms provide this avenue of escape for him.

The Aloof Dog—is worked just as the normal-average for this second day of teaching the stay.

The Shy-afraid Dog—should be worked as the normal-average on this second day of stays. The differences should continue to be *effusive* praise on your return, and even slight verbal praise while you are returning, to build up the dog's confidence. This dog can even be praised verbally while you are walking at heel if you feel his excessive apprehension warrants it.

The Fear-biter,
The Aggressive Dog—These dogs should be worked as the normal-average. Continue the hand signal in close proximity to your body. Praise verbally only. If they appear up-tight and stiff to you, you can also praise verbally as you are returning. Work your dog in a calm, precise manner. Never make jerky, excited movements or use vocal inflections. You would only serve to increase his apprehension and aggressive tendencies. Do not be afraid if your dog appears nervous when you introduce a new procedure into the routine. As the new work is repeated, and learned more thoroughly, you will notice your dog becoming more relaxed and confident, both in himself and in you. This is precisely what you are aiming to achieve. The usual two 15-minute sessions, with the accompanying five-minute breaks on the long line, will end this second day of stays for your dog.

THE THIRD DAY

The Normal-average Dog—Begin working your dog as usual with the complete routine as a warm up. Then come to a stop, put him on a stay, and leave him by stepping out one foot away. Wait five seconds, return to the heel position, take up the leash, and praise him. After a couple of stops where your dog is praised for just sitting, come to a stop and leave him on a stay. This time you will leave differently. You will give the STAY command as usual, with the left hand in front of your dog's face. Then leave your dog by confidently walking away from him, letting out the full six feet of the leash behind you. When you reach the end of the six feet, slowly turn and face your dog. Stand facing your dog and remain mo-

STAY SIGNAL AND COMMAND

WALKING OUT TO FULL 6 FEET OF LEASH

OUT IN FRONT AT FULL 6 FEET

tionless as you count off three seconds. Be certain not to exert any pressure on the leash; it must be slack. Then smoothly return to the heel position at your dog's side, take up the leash with the proper hand grip, and praise him. Then move on with a new HEEL command.

If your dog chooses to break the Sit-Stay by getting up and attempting to walk away—while you are leaving him on the stay, when you are out at the six-foot distance on the leash, or as you are returning to his side at heel position—you should correct him in the following manner. In order to break the Sit-Stay, before the dog can walk away from the spot he has been sitting on, he must first stand up from the sit position. It is at this precise moment, as his rear end is lifted up off the floor, that he must be corrected—not later, after he has taken several steps away from you or in your direction. As his rear comes off the floor and as he attempts to break, even before he has a chance to take the first step in any direction, you should promptly correct from wherever you are with a sharp jerk and release on the leash, accompanied by a simultaneous verbal NO. The correction should not propel your dog toward you. It should be so quick, in a sharp jerk and release motion, that your dog sits right back down on the very spot that he attempted to move from. The correction is a very quick jerk and release rather than a pulling or tugging motion. In this way you will be able to correct your dog from the full six feet away. After the correction, if your dog is still not sitting, he should receive a new SIT-STAY command, with the appropriate hand signal. You should alternate in this way with correction, command, correction, command, until you win out and he is sitting. You can then return to the dog's side and praise him.

Remember, you are correcting at precisely the same moment that he attempts to break the stay. This could be as you are leaving him on a stay, while you are out at the full six feet, or upon your return to heel position. This will teach your dog that you don't need to be on top of him to correct him, and realizing this is what will make his stay very secure.

If, upon your return, your dog gets up before you praise him, you will have to correct him with the usual jerk and release, coupled with the word NO. It is very undesirable to have to correct a dog that has successfully maintained a Sit-Stay, and chooses to break on your return. There are certain techniques that will help you to keep him sitting as you return. Don't run back to your dog's side quickly, taking up the leash with a quick, excited, jerking motion. This will only tend to make him get up, and would, really, almost not be his fault. Instead, as you return to the dog, slow down your pace, and move to his side with a slow, controlled motion. Similarly, take up the leash in the same calm, methodical fashion. Your dog should tend to emulate your controlled attitude on

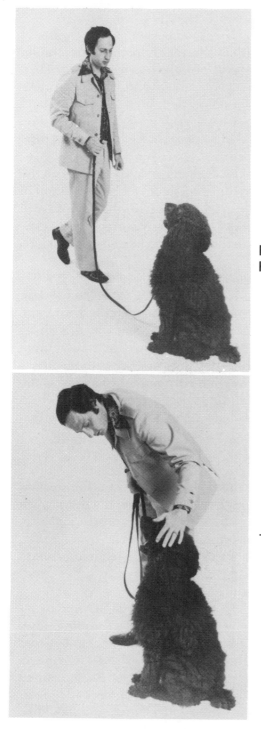

RETURNING SLOWLY TO
HEEL POSITION

TAKE UP LEASH
AND PRAISE

your return, and this will help to keep him sitting.

The way you return to your dog is very important, and the order in which you do things upon your return is also very important. You should first return to your dog's side at heel position, with him on your left. Then take up the leash slowly, with the proper hand grip, and, finally, praise your dog. Remember, once he has been praised, he is allowed to stand up, so make sure you have the proper leash grip before you praise; then you are ready to move on immediately to a new HEEL command should he get up while you are praising him.

The basic method employed in this training is slowly to build up the dog on the stays, instead of making him stay for an extended period of time and hanging him or correcting him when he breaks the stay. We will try to accomplish the teaching process with as few corrections as possible, and then we can justify firm corrections once he fully understands what is expected of him.

Move on to a new HEEL command and work your dog on a few automatic sits. Then, try a Sit-Stay, leaving your dog for five seconds at the full six feet. Return in the proper manner, take up the leash, and praise. Do not try any stays longer than five seconds at this time. Continue working on the heeling, sits, and Sit-Stays, for both 15-minute periods of this day's training. Give your dog the usual five-minute breaks on the long line, in distractions, between the two work sessions and at the end. Take him to the front or back of the house, depending upon which location provides greater distractions. However it is very important that there are NO distractions during today's *work* sessions.

The Overfriendly Dog,
The High-strung Dog—These dogs should be worked just as the normal-average, except that special attention should be given to the return with these dogs as they are most likely to break upon your return. Smooth, controlled returns, as previously described for the normal-average dog, will produce maximum results with these dogs. If they should break in spite of everything you do, you should correct in the usual way: NO, with a jerk, and then repeat the commands SIT, STAY.

Another danger spot with dogs in these two categories is their inability to accept praise in a rational way. They overreact to the praise, jumping all over you or attempting to run away. This can be counteracted by quickly praising your dog verbally only, and immediately moving on to a new HEEL command. As this is repeated, he will see that he cannot take advantage of you and will not attempt his wild antics any longer. Later on, as he is able to accept your praise with control, you should be

SIT-STAY CORRECTION:
JERK AND RELEASE WITH
VERBAL "NO"

EW COMMAND AND HAND
SIGNAL: "SIT," "STAY"

163

able to increase the verbal praise and even give some physical praise as well. By your dog's actions you can judge how much praise he should receive. If he goes wild, or jumps all over you, cut down the praise to a level where he no longer reacts in this manner.

Train your dog for the usual two 15-minute sessions without distractions, followed by the two five-minute breaks on the long line, with distractions.

The Aloof Dog—should be worked as the normal-average dog, and corrected forcefully if he attempts to break. This dog, in particular, may look away from you when you give the STAY command. This might lead you to believe that you should give the hand signal to accomodate where he happens to be looking. Wrong! Your responsibility is to give the command, and his is to see it. So don't worry where your dog is looking. If he doesn't stay, just correct firmly. Your dog may also look away while on the Sit-Stay, or perhaps even face the other direction. Give your commands and make your corrections as if your dog were watching you, and eventually he will be. Remember, he doesn't get corrected for looking away, but for getting up from the stay.

Work your dog in the usual two 15-minute sessions with no distractions, followed by the two five-minute breaks on the long line, in distractions. This will end the third day on the Sit-Stay for this dog.

The Shy-afraid Dog—should be treated just as the normal-average dog. It is very important that you do not put this dog in the position of being corrected on the Sit-Stay. Leave him for only three seconds, thereby building his confidence and minimizing corrections. If this dog starts to shake nervously, move, or lie down as you start to return, a very quiet, reassuring, VERY GOOD, JUST RELAX, will help to allay his fears as you return. The reassuring sound of your voice will build his confidence, rather than the silence that allows him to succumb to his innate fear. Once you reach his side, he should be lavishly praised both physically and verbally. Whether your dog is shy and afraid because of his breeding or because of mistreatment, he is probably most afraid when someone approaches close to him, and your return from the stay will be an anxious moment for him. As your return, with the accompanying praise, is repeated, your dog's confidence will grow and this will begin to change his attitude. In each case, with each different command, be it SIT, STAY, DOWN, or HEEL, the important thing is not only teaching your dog the mechanics of each command, but doing it in such a way as to improve the

164

dog's attitude favorably and change his personality more toward the normal-average.

Work your dog for the usual two 15-minute sessions, without distractions, followed by the two five-minute breaks, in distractions. This ends the third day of the Sit-Stay, for the shy-afraid dog.

The Fear-biter,
The Aggressive Dog—should be worked as the shy-afraid dog. This will mean praising verbally as you return. These dogs' problems, in almost all cases, have been caused by abuse rather than inferior breeding, so they will be especially apprehensive as you return from the stay. Together with soft verbal praise as you draw near, your hands should be carried low as you approach your dog. Approach slowly and return to your dog in the following manner: instead of approaching directly in line with your dog and swinging into heel position, make a wide swing and bypass your dog, making him feel you are going to walk right past him, and then smoothly and slowly return to heel position. This will minimize the dog's fears about your return and, in this way, build up his confidence and trust in you. Both dogs will be praised physically as soon as possible. Being able to be touched shows a beginning in attitude improvement.

Work these dogs for two 15-minute sessions without distractions, followed by the two five-minute breaks on the long line, with distractions. This ends the third day on the stay for these dogs.

THE FOURTH DAY

The Normal-average Dog—Bring your dog into the training area. Start working him in his general routine of heeling, automatic sits, and right and left turns, reviewing everything he knows. After a few minutes, when he is warmed up and working well, come to a stop. Give the STAY command and signal, and leave your dog, taking off on your right foot. Walk to the full six-foot length of the leash, turn and face him. After 15 seconds return to the heel position at your dog's side, take up the leash with the proper hand position, and *then* praise your dog. Again move on with a new HEEL command, taking off on your left foot. We will follow the basic rule that every time we want the dog to walk with us we will take off on our left foot—the reason being that this is the foot closest to him when at correct heel position, and he can notice it more easily. When we want the dog to stay, we would leave him by taking off starting with our right foot, which is farthest from him, making it less likely that he would move out with us.

165

On your next stop, just praise your dog when he sits, then move on with a new HEEL command. Come to a stop, and when your dog sits give the STAY command and leave him in the usual manner. Remember to give the command and signals properly and with the proper timing. You are prefacing *all* commands with your dog's name: Dream, STAY. The hand signal is given simultaneously as you speak his name, then the word STAY follows as you maintain the stay signal with your hand. After you have told him to stay, your hand is dropped to your side. You should not maintain the hand signal, repeating STAY commands, STAY, STAY, STAY, and begging your dog to comply. Leave, walking the full six feet away, turn around and face your dog for 15 seconds. If your dog should break, correct him from the full six feet away with a sharp jerk and release, coupled with the word NO! Then return to his side, take up the leash, and praise him. Continue working the dog, alternating every other stop with a Sit-Stay. All Sit-Stays should be 15 seconds in duration, correcting when necessary. The session should be the normal 15 minutes, but note, there should be no distractions on this fourth day of the Sit-Stay.

Give your dog the usual five-minute break on the long line, with distractions. Then begin working your dog as before, except that the length of the stays should be increased to 25 seconds. Work your dog for a second 15-minute session, followed by another five-minute break on the long line, in distractions.

The Overfriendly Dog,
The High-strung Dog—Work these dogs as the normal-average, being careful not to overpraise. Give them only as much praise as they can handle. Remember to move out on your right foot after having given the STAY command and signal. After returning to your dog, take up the leash, then praise him. When giving a new HEEL command, you should take off on your left foot, the one closest to the dog.

Work your dog for one 15-minute session, on his whole routine, using 15-second stays, followed by a five-minute break on the long line, in distractions. The second session should be the same as the first, except that the stays are increased to 25 seconds. Work your dog without distractions for both sessions, and introduce distractions only on the breaks.

The Aloof Dog—is worked as the normal-average, except that you must be sure to give your commands and signals in the proper way. Sometimes these dogs will renew their stubbornness, when walking with you, as

166

TAKING OFF ON LEFT FOOT FOR HEELING

TAKING OFF ON RIGHT FOOT FOR "THE STAY"

something new is presented to them. Your reaction to his apparent lack of desire to continue the lesson is to cope with it as you did in the beginning, by running when needed and continuing to teach the stay, showing him that his resistance cannot deter you as he hopes it will. This dog, more than any other, can try your practice and make you lose your temper. This is exactly what he wants and, if he can make you angry enough to break your routine, then he will consider himself the victor. To best him you must outlast him, by continuing to work him in the proper way consistently, and never allowing him to make you lose your temper. If the things he is trying on you are not successful, then he will give them up.

Work your dog for two 15-minute sessions without distractions, on his complete routine. Follow each session with the usual five-minute break on the 20-foot line, in distractions. On the first session you should work 15-second stays. With the second session the stay increases to 25 seconds.

The Shy-afraid Dog—This dog should also be worked as the normal-average. The repetitions of the entire routine will begin to make him more confident. It is important to correct this dog firmly, because we want to transfer his fear of other things to the correction. In this way, his fear of the correction will overpower his fear of other things, and enable us to work him in those other areas, gradually bringing about a positive change of character. Contrary to popular belief, this dog should not be coddled, which, in his mind, only justifies his fears. He should be trained in a positive way and given plenty of praise when he does the right thing.

Work him for two 15-minute sessions without distractions, followed by the two five-minute breaks on the 20-foot line, in distractions. The first session should have 15-second stays. On the second session you should lengthen the time to 25 seconds.

The Fear-biter,
The Aggressive Dog—These dogs should be worked basically as the normal-average. The use of the hand signal on the stay can be gradually increased in boldness. Since it is a threatening gesture to your dog, as you are able to increase the proximity of the hand signal to his face his trust in you is growing, and you are beginning to change his attitude favorably. This must be done very gradually. If corrections are necessary on the stay for these dogs, you may correct them, but the corrections must be followed immediately by verbal praise. Continue to increase the physical

praise as your dog is able to accept more. If your dog appears up-tight on your return, verbally praise him as you draw near. As he becomes more confident you can omit this verbal praise while returning, and just give physical and verbal praise after you have returned.

Work these dogs for the usual two 15-minute sessions, followed by the two five-minute breaks. The stays will be 15 seconds during the first session and increase to 25 seconds for the second session. Work without distractions, but give the breaks with distractions. This ends the fourth day of stays for these dogs.

THE FIFTH DAY

The Normal-average Dog—Begin working your dog in the usual manner, then leave him on a stay for 45 seconds. Continue working your dog, and on the next stay return after ten seconds. You should now begin to vary the length of the stays, and the purpose is so that your dog doesn't know how long he is going to have to maintain the stay. He must come to realize that he must stay no matter how long or short the time, and he is released only when you return and praise him. After working your dog for five minutes on the above routine, you should begin to introduce a small distraction on the stays, which you yourself will provide. After leaving your dog on a stay in the usual manner, instead of standing motionless, facing him from the full six feet away, try taking one or two steps sideways, first to your left and then to your right. You should wind up approximately in the center, still facing your dog. You should then return in the usual manner, take up the leash, and praise him. On the next stay you should introduce a soft whistle, and then return and praise him. Work your dog on a few more automatic sits. Then prepare for another Sit-Stay. This time you should introduce both distractions from the last stays, moving back and forth and whistling softly, in addition to a new distraction, the snapping of your fingers lightly a couple of times. Alternate all three distractions on one 45-second stay, then return in the usual manner and praise your dog.

Many people call their dogs to them by snapping their fingers, whistling, or slapping their hand against their leg. Since these sounds can be made by anyone, your dog must learn to completely ignore them and not respond to these sounds, whether made by his owners or by an utter stranger. The only way you will ever call your dog to you will be by giving the correct verbal command, which will be learned later on. All other inviting sounds must be completely ignored by him. If you have, in the past, called your dog to you by any of these means, you must stop

169

doing so from now on. These sounds will hereafter build in intensity, and be used only as distractions for your dog to ignore. As you are working your dog, if he should attempt to break the stay, give him a very hard correction and continue building up the distractions until he grows in reliability and can ignore them with ease.

Some day in the future, because of circumstances beyond your control, you may have your dog off the leash and have the need to leave him on a Sit-Stay. He may be sitting at a curb along a heavily trafficked street, with someone on the other side of the street whistling or snapping his fingers. If the dog breaks and runs into the traffic, he will die. All that holds him there is the memory of your corrections. Make sure your dog remembers that they were very, very hard.

After 15 minutes of the above workout, give your dog a five-minute break on the long line, in distractions. Then work your dog for another 15 minutes, varying the time of stays from ten seconds to 45 seconds so that he does not anticipate a routine. In addition, vary the distractions you used for the first session, building them in frequency as well as intensity. Give your dog his final break on the 20-foot line, in distractions. This ends the fifth day of stays for the normal-average dog.

The Overfriendly Dog,
The High-strung Dog—These dogs should be worked basically as the normal-average dog, the exceptions being that they must be built up much more slowly on the distractions and given abundant praise upon your return. This will show them that they have made the right choice.

For dogs in this class, distractions are their weakest spots and they are looking for any excuse to break their stay. Your distractions provide the ultimate temptation for them. If they do break, you must correct very firmly. Take your time and build up the distractions very gradually.

Work your dog for two 15-minute sessions without distractions. Then give him two five-minute breaks on the 20-foot line, in distractions.

The Aloof Dog—For the Sit-Stays, the aloof dog can be handled as the normal-average. You will very likely incur the problem of his consistently breaking the Sit-Stay. He is trying to convince you that he is confused and doesn't understand, hoping that you'll give up. The truth is that he knows exactly what you want but is hoping you will not be able to enforce your wishes. He is searching for an area of weakness on your part. Don't let him find it. Correct him repeatedly, as needed; make the corrections very hard and, at the same time, emotionless. Your job in this case is to emulate a cold, uncompromising machine. With such a machine he will not be able to argue. You must outlast him and beat him at his own game. In all other respects, treat him and work him as the normal-average dog. This means two 15-minute sessions without distractions, and two five-minute breaks on the long line, in distractions.

The Shy-afraid Dog—This dog should be worked like the overfriendly and high-strung dogs in that you should build up distractions slowly so that corrections are minimal. This dog is usually very willing to please if you only approach him with a gentle consistency. Building up distractions too quickly (whistling, finger snapping, etc.), thereby triggering the accompanying corrections, will only serve to break down this dog's confidence and cause a regression in training. He will construe the corrections as abuse by you, and retreat back into his shell. Nurture this dog slowly, making a series of positive victories for both you and the dog. The extra time spent will be well worth the reliability of performance, and, more important, the change of attitude in your dog toward the normal-average.

Work your dog for two 15-minute sessions without distractions, followed by two five-minute breaks on the 20-foot line, in distractions.

IN AN EMERGENCY, YOUR DOG'S MEMORY OF YOUR
SEVERE CORRECTIONS WILL SAVE HIS LIFE

The Fear-biter,
The Aggressive Dog—Work these dogs as the overfriendly and the high-strung dogs. This means building up the distractions very, very slowly, requiring minimal corrections. Should you find that your dog requires frequent corrections, then take an extra day or two to build up the distractions (moving left and right, snapping fingers, and whistling) very, very slowly. After this extra time bring your dog back into the normal routine. Whenever something new is being taught to dogs in this category, they interpret the unknown as a threat to themselves. This, in turn, causes a temporary setback in their confidence in you. To help allay this renewed mistrust, you should continue mixing the old, well-learned routine of just praising him for his automatic sits, without doing stays for a while, and alternate with the new routine of the stays. This provides the opportunity for praise, by reviewing well-learned past commands, and will help your dog to make a less traumatic transition from old to new material.

Two sessions of 15 minutes, plus the two five-minute breaks on the long line, with distractions, will end the fifth day of stays for these dogs.

THE SIXTH DAY

The Normal-average Dog—With a controlled distraction at one end of the training area, such as someone clanging two pot lids together, or a tied-up or staked-out dog or cat, enter the training area from the opposite side. Begin working your dog in his heeling routine with right- and left-angle turns, about-turns, and stops where you just praise him for doing the automatic sit. When he is warmed up and working well, make a stop at least 20 feet from the distraction. Leave your dog by giving the proper STAY command and hand signal. Face him from the six-foot length of the leash, and after ten seconds return and praise him. Note that you have not yourself provided any distraction, but are making use of the distraction behind you.

Begin working your dog toward the distraction on everything but stays, moving closer and then away. Continue this until your dog is working very well; then prepare for your next stop, which will be a Sit-Stay. Whether you had to correct or not, once your dog is working well, leave him on a Sit-Stay, ten feet from the distraction and walk to the full six feet of the leash. Wait ten seconds, then return and praise. It would be unfortunate if you would have to correct your dog at this time, but, if he should get up, you must correct from wherever you are when he breaks. If, after the correction, your dog still does not assume the sit position, give a new command, Dream, SIT, STAY, and show him the correct hand signal from a distance. If he is still not sitting, give another leash correction and continue alternating correction with command until you win out. It is very important that you realize that you *do not* have to return to your dog to correct him. It is important that he realizes this also.

Begin working your dog again, toward and away from the distraction. At some ten feet from the distraction, give a STAY command and walk out to the full six feet away. Return after 30 seconds, take up the leash and praise. When working your dog on the Sit-Stay, be sure to stand at the side farthest from the distraction, so that your dog is between you and the distraction. Continue working your dog and, after a few stops of just automatic sits, leave your dog for another 30-second Sit-Stay. Return and praise. Work your dog in his complete routine for the remainder of this first 15-minute session. With the distractions still present, give your dog a five-minute break on the long line, at the area opposite to the distraction.

SIT-STAY WITH AT ONE
END DISTRACTION

After the break, again begin working your dog in his complete routine and, after a warm-up, leave him on a Sit-Stay, about ten feet from the distraction. Make this first one a 30-second stay. Return, take up the leash, and praise. Continue working your dog closer to the distraction until you are only three to four feet away. Come to a stop, leave your dog on a stay for ten seconds, return, take up the leash, and praise. If corrections are necessary, make them very, very hard. After a few more right-about turns, automatic sits, etc., make another stop three or four feet from the distraction. Leave for 20 seconds, return, and praise. Repeat the routine, moving close, then away, and again leave your dog on a Sit-Stay three or four feet from the distraction, this time for 30 seconds. Work your dog on Sit-Stays both close to and far from the distractions. Also, vary the length of time on the stays, with up to a 30-second maximum. Continue working your dog in the above routine for the remainder of this work session. Afterwards give your dog the usual five-minute break on the 20-foot line, with the distraction still present. This will end the stay for the sixth day for the normal-average dog.

The Overfriendly Dog,
The High-strung Dog—These dogs should be worked as the normal-average, except that at no time during the first work session should you get closer than 20 feet from the distraction. After the break, which will be on the 20-foot clothesline with the distraction still present, go back for the second session. Then the dog can be worked closer to the distraction, first at ten feet and finally working as close as three or four feet. Remember to correct hard when needed, and give as much praise as your particular dog can handle. Take the final break and end the session for this day.

The Aloof Dog—will be handled as the normal-average, except correcting very hard when needed. Your dog should be between you and the distraction on the stays. He may turn facing the distractions completely. This is satisfactory as long as he doesn't break the stay. Continue doing the right thing no matter what your dog does; don't allow him to make you angry or flustered.

Work the usual two 15-minute sessions, with the distraction at one end of the area. Have the distraction remain on the breaks.

The Shy-afraid Dog—Work the shy-afraid dog as the overfriendly and high-strung dogs. Build up the distractions very slowly, trying to correct as little as possible. When you return, give plenty of praise, making the session a very positive experience for your dog.

Work the two 15-minute sessions, advancing toward the distractions as with the overfriendly and high-strung dogs. Give the breaks on the 20-foot line, with the distractions still present.

The Fear-biter,
The Aggressive Dog—These dogs should be worked as the normal-

average, with the exceptions that, in the first 15-minute session, you should not get closer than 20 feet to the distraction and the stays should be only ten seconds. In the second session you should be no closer than 20 feet from the distractions again, but the stays should be 20-seconds long. If your dog falls into these categories, work him for an extra day or two on these distractions, building up very slowly, until you can take him through the same routine as the normal-average dog for this sixth day. These dogs, especially the aggressive dog, may be able to justify trying to bite you when you try to stop them from going for the distraction. This is why the teaching process must be longer for them. Building them up slowly enables them to accept your corrections, instead of choosing to contest them with aggression.

Work your dog for the usual two 15-minute sessions and the five-minute breaks on the 20-foot line. After your extra days' work, resume the regular schedule for the seventh day of stays.

THE SEVENTH DAY

The Normal-average Dog—When you enter the training area, it should be full of assorted distractions such as people, animals, etc. Begin working your dog on heeling and automatic sits, until you have gained his full attention. Come to a stop five feet from a distraction. If your dog does not sit immediately, administer a very hard correction. Heel him off, make an about-turn and come back to within five feet of the same distraction, again making your stop in the same place. Continue making stops near this distraction until your dog ignores it completely and does a quick automatic sit every time. Only then is he ready for a stay, near the distraction. Leave your dog on a stay in the proper fashion. Walk six feet away and stand facing him from the six-foot length of the leash. After 30 seconds return to his side, take up the leash, and praise him GOOD BOY. Then move off with a new HEEL command.

You should have three or more distractions throughout the training area. Approach the next distraction, working your dog on automatic sits. When he is working well, leave him on another stay, again for 30 seconds. Return, take up the leash, and praise. If your dog breaks any of the stays, be sure to handle it in the usual manner with very hard corrections. Approach another distraction and again leave your dog on a Sit-Stay, for a full minute. For the rest of this session continue making stops five feet from each distraction, but begin varying the time of the stays, either ten seconds, 30 seconds, or one minute. Continue this routine for the first 15-minute session, then give him a break on the 20-foot line, not letting him make contact with any of the distractions, and correcting if he attempts to.

After the five-minute break, snap on the leash, snap off the line, make another stop five feet from a distraction, and leave him on a stay. With your dog on the stay, lightly snap your fingers, pat your thigh, and whistle softly. After 15 seconds, return, take up the leash, and praise your dog, showing him that he was correct in ignoring the distractions, including ones you yourself made. Heel him off again, making a stop five feet from a distraction. Give a STAY command and signal. While you are out on the stay, increase the intensity and frequency of your self-made distractions. This time maintain the stay for 30 seconds. Return, take up the leash, and praise. Continue working this 15-minute session and building up the self-made distractions while working among the external distractions. You should build up to a full minute on the stays, correcting whenever your dog breaks and starting again at a lower level, to be built up once again as he is able to handle it.

Never allow your dog to make contact with a distraction when working or when on a break. Should he do so, it will be much harder for you to command his attention afterwards. Continue working your dog as close as five feet from the distractions, varying the time on stays among 10, 30, and 60 seconds. Also vary the intensity and frequency of self-made distractions, so your dog can never anticipate a set routine. Work the second 15-minute session and then give a final break on the 20-foot line, with distractions still present. This will end the seventh day on the Sit-Stay for the normal-average dog.

Your dog will be learning the down next. In order to have a really effective down, the Sit-Stay must be very secure. At this point, feel free to work your dog for an extra day or two on the Sit-Stay. It will make fair dogs good and good dogs even better. Your dog must be able to work at the level described above, before you attempt to teach him the more difficult down that follows.

The Overfriendly Dog,

The High-strung Dog—These two dogs should be worked as the normal-average, taking care to build up very slowly the distractions that you make. If forced to correct, go back into the same distractions, but omit your self-made diversions. After one or two stays without your own distractions, you may reintroduce them, building him up slowly again. Build these dogs to the reliable level described for the normal-average dog. Take an extra day or two on the stays to make them more secure, if needed, in preparation for the down to follow.

The Aloof Dog—Work this dog as the normal-average, consistently correcting hard when needed. If your dog slows down to look at a distraction behind him, correct him by breaking into a run for a few yards. Make sure your dog is reliable on the stays before moving on to the more difficult down that follows.

The Shy-afraid Dog—Work this dog as the normal-average, but build him up slowly and give ample praise when justified.

The Fear-biter,
The Aggressive Dog—Work these dogs as the normal-average, with the exception that the first two stays will be no closer than 20 feet from the distraction. Build up until you can get as close as five feet, and build in all respects to the level of the normal-average dog. Go back and reread this day's training for the normal-average dog. It is very important that these dogs be working at the level described for the normal-average before attempting to teach the down which follows. When leaving him on the stays, be sure that your dog is between you and the distraction so that, if he breaks, he cannot make physical contact with it.

When your dog can reliably sit and stay five feet from a distraction, then he will be ready to learn the hardest command of all for you and for him, the DOWN.

THE DOWN

The DOWN command will be a specific command that will mean to your dog that you want him to lie down prone on the ground. It will be used in conjunction with the command STAY, and a Down-Stay will be the most effective way of controlling your dog in times of maximum excitement and possible danger. Because the Down-Stay is comfortable, your dog can hold this position for a very long time. This command, the DOWN, will be the most difficult of all for your dog to learn. The reason for this is that dogs consider the act of lying down as complete submission to an opponent. In a dog fight, if the loser lies down and submits, he can often save himself further injury or death by so doing. Usually a severe beating must be administered by his dog opponent to make a loser dog lie down in this way. Therefore, when commanding your dog to lie down, you are asking much more, in *his* mind, than just another command. With this knowledge in *your* mind, special techniques will be used that the authors have found to be most effective and least punitive from the dog's point of view. The command DOWN will mean to your dog that

THE DOWN

you want him to lie down immediately at your command. To avoid any possible confusion in his mind, and to keep things simplest for him, we will use the DOWN command only when we want our dog to lie down, and not when we want him to get off a couch or stop jumping on someone. For all these other transgressions we will use the word NO. In that way the DOWN will not be a reprimand, but just another command that will not be as offensive to him or as hard to take from you.

Teaching the down will be accomplished in two distinct phases. The first part will consist of physically placing him in the down position, while at the same time giving the command, Dream, DOWN. The second phase will consist of correcting the dog for not lying down, and proving to him that you can not only correct him if he refuses to lie down, but that you can physically knock him to the ground each time he refuses to obey your DOWN command.

There are many diverse methods for teaching a dog to lie down—they vary among professional dog trainers. Most of these methods consist of the basic technique of applying a downward pressure on the leash with either the trainer's hand or foot, and gradually increasing the pressure as the command DOWN is given, until the pressure causes the struggling dog finally to submit and lie down. The amount of punishment that some dogs take as they resist the downward pressure employed with this method is excessive beyond need and, with very stubborn dogs, greatly intensified. It is harder to teach some dogs the down than others, but the

178

amount of punishment they must receive when learning the down can be greatly minimized by using the more positive method that follows.

Since we are fighting the dog's natural tendency to resist us, and since this command will be most distasteful to the dog, we want to make the teaching method as pleasant as possible for him. There is no way a dog can enjoy or even passively tolerate having someone step on his leash or apply manual pressure to slowly pull him to the ground. However, contrast this with our method, which will be, gently, with your left hand on his back and your right hand holding his front paws, to place him in the down position and praise him lavishly as soon as he is lying down. Our teaching or placing process will last for five days, so your dog will have all this time to learn what DOWN means before ever being corrected for not lying down. When he finally is corrected, he will be given very strong corrections in a *downward* direction, in a special way that will knock him off his feet, causing him to lie down. In the other methods, corrections, after ten or 15 minutes of choking the dog into the down position, are made in an upward direction each time the dog refuses to lie down when commanded. At this time you may ask yourself, "Isn't this exactly like a sit correction? Won't this make my dog think I want him to sit, thereby confusing him?" The answer is "Yes," which is precisely why we correct for the down in a downward direction. It leaves no doubt in the dog's mind as to what is expected of him. We will now proceed with the actual teaching of the down.

THE FIRST DAY

The Normal-average Dog—Enter the training area with your dog. Make sure there are no distractions in the area. Begin working your dog on the entire routine, including automatic sits, Sit-Stays, heeling, etc. When he is warmed up and working well, come to a stop. As soon as he does his automatic sit, place him down in the following manner. With the leash held entirely in your right hand, place your left hand on his head as if to praise him. Drop the leash to the ground from your right hand (the leash is laid out in front of you, where you can easily step on it or grab it if the need arises). Run your left hand down your dog's neck, stopping in the middle of his back, placing the open palm of your hand on his back. Then bend forward and, with your right hand, reach under his front legs. Reach with your right hand twisted forward, knuckles down, palm upward, thumb pointed in the direction the dog is facing. With your right hand, reach under the foot closest to you and grab the second foot, which is the dog's left front foot. Next, the front legs are lifted slightly and

179

pushed forward while, at the same time, you exert downward pressure on the dog's back with your left hand. As your dog is reaching the down position, speak the command, Dream, DOWN. The emphasis is on the word DOWN, which is much louder and drawn out than the word that precedes it. As soon as your dog is down, lavishly praise him, giving as much praise as he can handle. Then grab the leash near his neck with your right hand and move off with a new HEEL command, taking up the proper hand grip and straightening out the leash as you walk.

Dogs are great natural students of body language. They are very aware of the way other animals and people move. If you want your dog to trust you and be confident in what you are doing, you must move smoothly and surely into each maneuver and so impart to your dog the belief that you are indeed quite confident and capable. To accomplish this, you must be thoroughly familiar with the movements required of you as you place your dog down. Study the accompanying photos carefully and try to visualize the specific movements before actually applying the techniques to your dog. The placement method as described above will be used on all breeds with the exception of some of the very small toy breeds. The method for those dogs will be modified slightly. Instead of reaching in with your right hand and grabbing a leg, since the dog is so small, you will just have room enough to reach in with one or two fingers behind his front legs. Then push forward, as your left hand pushes down on his back, sweeping him to the ground, where he is immediately praised. Continue working your dog on heeling, do a Sit-Stay or two, then, as you're heeling him, come to a stop. As he sits, move in quickly and place him down. Remember to say the word DOWN louder than your dog's name. Also, make the command long and drawn out, DOOWWWN! It is important to note that your dog should not be placed down repeatedly, again and again, but, instead, the routine should be varied so that he cannot predict any regular order to your routine. Never do two downs in a row; always a down, then a Sit-Stay or some heeling with automatic sits before doing another down. Work your dog on this routine throughout the first 15-minute session, then give him his usual break on the 20-foot clothesline, in distractions. After the break bring him back for an exact repetition of the first 15-minute session, including review of all his other work. After the second session give him his final break and leave the area, ending the first day's session on the down.

The Overfriendly Dog,
The High-strung Dog—should be worked as the normal-average. These dogs will anticipate what you are doing, after they have been placed

down one or two times, and will quickly move to block your initial grab for them. Your best counter for this is to mix up the routine so they never know when you are going to do the down, and move in on them very quickly when you do place them down. These dogs also may present a problem by fouling the leash, either purposely or accidentally or both, after they are placed down. They may roll over on their backs and tangle the leash around one or both of their front paws. To counteract this, with your right hand simply grab the leash near the dog's neck, where it meets his collar, and, giving a new HEEL command, walk away as you take up the leash with the proper hand grip. Although very friendly, these dogs are attempting to put a stop to your routine of placing them down by fouling the leash, thereby causing you to struggle with them and the leash as you try to unravel the leash from their feet.

Another protest may take the form of his mouthing your right hand immediately after he reaches the down position. He is not biting you, he is just holding on. It is his way of telling you he doesn't like what you are doing and would like you to stop. He is hoping, once again, to break up your routine by getting you excited. The best way to stop this is simply to remove your right hand, a split second before he touches the ground. Swing it out and down near your right hip, leaving him nothing to bite. If you practice this maneuver a few times, you will be able to take your dog down, and have your right hand by your side by the time he hits the ground. The last form of half-protest that these dogs may attempt is to roll over completely on their backs and paw the air. Rolling over on their backs, after being placed down in the beginning, is okay, and your dog still gets praised for lying down. But if he rolls over in a wild frantic manner, you must stop this immediately by grabbing the leash near his neck and quickly moving off with a new HEEL command.

Vary the routine, and work these dogs for the usual two 15-minute sessions, without distractions, after which you should give them the usual two breaks on the 20-foot line, in distractions.

The Aloof Dog—is worked as the normal-average. He may renew his resistance to walking with you. This should be counteracted by your running when you start to heel him. He may also try to mouth you as you place him down. You should remove your right hand quickly, before your dog hits the ground, so that it is out of his way and unable to provide the interuption in routine that he is hoping for.

Work your dog for two 15-minute sessions, without distractions. Then give him his two five-minute breaks on the 20-foot line, in distractions.

181

DROPPING LEASH, LEFT
HAND PRAISING

REACHING UNDER FRONT FEET

182

SWEEPING OUT FRONT,
PRESSURE ON BACK

DOG DOWN, BEING PRAISED

The Shy-afraid Dog—should be worked as the normal-average, except that he should be prepared for the down placement, rather than directly placing him down. To prepare your dog for the down, leave him on a Sit-Stay. After a few seconds, return to his side. Stroke his side and legs, hesitate, then praise him. Make the next few stops just Sit-Stays, where you will return and touch him lightly, hesitating, and then praising him. After about six or seven of these touching maneuvers, your dog will be ready to be placed down gently. He will be placed as the normal-average, and given abundant praise once he is down.

Work this dog for the usual two 15-minute sessions, without distractions, followed by the two five-minute breaks on the 20-foot line, in distractions.

DOG DOWN, FOULING LEASH
GRAB NEAR NECK

The Fear-biter,
The Aggressive Dog—should be built up gradually with preliminary touching before going into placing them down. As these dogs are starting to go down, it is sometimes helpful if you praise them verbally before they touch the ground. This gets them over a worrisome moment. In all other ways, work these dogs exactly as the normal-average.

The two work sessions will be 15 minutes, without distractions, followed by the two five-minute breaks on the 20-foot line, in distractions.

THE SECOND DAY

The Normal-average Dog,
The Overfriendly Dog,
The High-strung Dog,
The Aloof Dog,
The Shy-afraid Dog,
The Fear-biter,
The Aggressive Dog—Work each of these dogs as they were worked on the first day of the down placement. Concentrate on building up the time on Sit-Stays to a minute and a half. Throughout the entire routine continue to place them down, alternating commands so as not to become predictable.

Work the two 15-minute sessions, without distractions. Give the five-minute breaks on the 20-foot line, in distractions.

THE THIRD DAY

The Normal-average Dog,
The Overfriendly Dog,
The High-strung Dog,
The Aloof Dog,
The Shy-afraid Dog,
The Fear-biter,
The Aggressive Dog—Work each of these dogs as they were worked on the first and second days of the down placement. By now you should be encountering less resistance as you place them down.

If, after a few days, you find your dog melting under you and almost lying down on the command, steps must be taken to prevent him from doing so at this time. You should continue to *place* him down, with your left hand on his back and your right hand sweeping his front legs forward, not allowing him to lie down on his OWN at this time. It is very important, and cannot be emphasized enough, that your dog must not be allowed to lie down on your command, without being properly placed down by you. If your dog were allowed to lie down at this point, you would never, in the future, have as reliable and immediate a down response as will be achieved by following the methods exactly as prescribed.

Work your dog for his usual two 15-minute sessions, without distractions, followed by the two five-minute breaks on the 20-foot line, in distractions.

THE FOURTH DAY

The Normal-average Dog,
The Overfriendly Dog,
The High-strung Dog,
The Aloof Dog,
The Shy-afraid Dog,
The Fear-biter,
The Aggressive Dog—Work each of these dogs as they were worked on the previous days of the down placement. It is advisable to place your dog down on a soft surface, such as the living room rug or a soft lawn. Do not send him crashing down on a hard cement surface, which will only serve to build up his resistance and apprehension. To make him more receptive to it, be considerate as to where you do your down placement. Also, be sure to move in quickly and securely. Don't allow your dog to anticipate your moves and wriggle away from you in resistance.

Work your dog for the usual two 15-minute sessions, without distractions, and then give him the two five-minute breaks on the 20-foot line, with distractions present.

THE FIFTH DAY

The Normal-average Dog,
The Overfriendly Dog,
The High-strung Dog,
The Aloof Dog,
The Shy-afraid Dog,
The Fear-biter,
The Aggressive Dog—This fifth day will probably be the last day of placing your dog down for most of them. Work each of these dogs as you did on the previous days. By this time your dog must allow himself to be placed down freely and easily by you. He should be very familiar with what you are doing, and should not be trying to contest it at all. If there remains any resistance on your dog's part to being placed down by you, then do NOT at this time go on to the sixth day's training routine. Instead, continue to place your dog on the down for an extra day or two, until he accepts the down freely.

Work your dog for the usual two 15-minute sessions, without distractions. Then give him the two five-minute breaks on the 20-foot line, in distractions. This will end the fifth day of the down for your dog.

THE SIXTH DAY

Today will be a memorable day for your dog. For the past five days we have been teaching him what the word DOWN means by physically placing him down. We can now assume that he knows what the word DOWN means and what is expected of him when given the DOWN command. From this point on, the teaching process ceases. You will never again place him down. You must just correct him every time he does not lie down at your command. These corrections are more powerful and different than any he has received previously.

It is very important, for this day's training session, that the dog be worked in an area completely free of distractions. If you don't have a suitable outside area, then the next best place to work your dog would be in a quiet room in the house. If you choose to work your dog inside, a smooth hard slippery surface will make things easier for both you and your dog.

The Normal-average Dog—Enter the training area and begin working your dog in his complete routine. When he is warmed up and working well, come to a stop and, as he does his automatic sit, turn to your left so that you are facing your dog and almost in front of him. Holding both hands on the leash and with the leash held slack, bend forward slightly and give the DOWN command: Dream, DOWN. Remain motionless for four seconds. There must be no tension whatsoever on the leash when you give the command. If your dog lies down, praise him, then move off with a new HEEL command. If he does not lie down, which is most often the case, after four seconds you should correct as follows: with both hands on the leash, approximately a foot and a half from the dog's neck (this varies with the size of the dog, smaller ones requiring less distance and larger ones requiring more), slowly move your hands toward the dog, then sharply move them in a downward, forceful, silent correction. This correction should be angled slightly to your left, which is also the dog's right front.

One such smooth, powerful correction, if properly administered, should knock your dog to the ground in the down position. As soon as your dog is in the down position, immediately step back to heel position and praise him lavishly. The reason why the correction is not directly in front of the dog, but is slightly to the side, is that, if the correction came from the front, he would be able to brace himself against it with both legs. But, delivered from the side, the force of the correction is exerted almost entirely on his right front foot, easily knocking him down.

187

It is important that you study the accompanying photos very carefully so that you may perform this maneuver correctly. If your dog is very big, or you have not done the correction properly, or, for any reason, were not able to knock him to the ground with your first correction, then, after four seconds, give him a new command, Dream, DOWN, and, four seconds later, a new, more powerful, silent correction. Once he is down, quickly step back to the heel position and praise him, moving off with a new HEEL command. If your dog still did not lie down for you after the second correction, then continue alternating commands with corrections until you finally win out either by knocking him down or having him give in and lie down for you. It doesn't matter whether you had to knock him down or he went down by himself, your dog should always get praised once he is in the down position. Make two more stops, where the dog is just praised for doing the automatic sit. Then, on the third stop, turn and face your dog, bowing forward slightly, and again give the DOWN command. After the four-second wait, if he has not gone down, get back to the heel position and immediately praise him, moving off with a new HEEL command. Continue working your dog, alternating among stays, automatic sits, and downs, until your dog is lying down at your DOWN command every time you give it.

Some dogs require only one or two down corrections, before they will give in and lie down at your command. Others may require as many as ten or more corrections. Occasionally, on rare instances, some dogs will require as many as 20 or 30 of these corrections before they will give in and lie down. No matter how many corrections your particular dog requires, whether it be two or 30, make sure that you provide them. You must have complete confidence in what you are doing and persevere until you win out. There is no doubt that your dog has been more than adequately prepared for these corrections, because you have placed him down for the previous five days.

You must continue the corrections until you win out; it is the only possible ending for this training session. It can only end with you winning out and him lying down. The normal 15-minute time limit will be waived for this particular phase because you won't stop until you win out. Once your dog gives in and lies down for you the first time, this does not mean that he will lie down for you every time. Therefore this is not the time to stop. He still may require more corrections. After you have four successive downs in a row, you can be confident that he has given in almost 100 percent and now deserves a break. The usual break on the 20-foot line, *with no distractions present*, should be given after this first training session.

COMMAND "DREAM,
DOWN!" FROM
THIS POSITION

BEGIN CORRECTION WITH
HANDS CLOSE TO DOG'S
FACE FOR MAXIMUM
DOWNWARD THRUST

189

DOWNWARD IMPACT KNOCKING DOG TO GROUND

DOG IN DOWN POSITION

DOG DOWNING AT HEEL POSITION

The second session should begin by warming your dog up with a couple of automatic sits. On the third stop, turn to your left, facing your dog, and give the DOWN command. If he lies down, step back to the heel position and praise him. If he chooses not to, let your correction leave no doubt that he has definitely made the wrong choice. Whether he lies down himself, or is knocked down by your correction, once he is down you should step back to the heel position and praise him. Continue working your dog, and again mix up the routine, doing a stay, an automatic sit, and then a down. Occasionally some dogs will renew their resistance during this second session. If this is the case with your dog, just continue to correct in the usual manner until you win out. This day's training sessions must end only one way, with you winning out and your dog lying down. The 15-minute time limit again will not apply, and you should not end this second session until you have gotten four successive downs from him. If you get the four downs in a row quickly, then you may end this second session after a few minutes. The usual five-minute break, *without distractions,* will end this day's training session.

191

Let's take a moment and review what you have done today, from your dog's angle. You have spent five days teaching him, in a very pleasant way, what the command DOWN meant. Two or three days would have been enough for almost any dog, but you gave him five full days—and both sessions each day. You left no doubt what the word DOWN meant to him. For a dog, knowing something does not mean he will always do it. Sometimes it takes a little more—sometimes he needs to know that you can always make him do what you want. After you taught him what DOWN meant, you then told him to lie down and, when he didn't, you showed him that you were capable of knocking him to the ground. You maintained consistency in that, every time he refused to comply, you proved your capabilities by again knocking him down. No matter how he got there, once he was down he always was praised. After today's training session your dog must have a new world of respect for you and your capabilities. Your dog will never forget what happened today, and his response to your DOWN commands in the future will be faster and better than you ever thought possible.

NOTE: Be certain that you never use the word DOWN, from this day forward, for anything other than when you want your dog to lie down. All other negative behavior, such as jumping on people or getting on furniture, will be handled with one word—NO.

The Overfriendly Dog,
The High-strung Dog—These dogs should be worked as the normal-average, except that when they are lying down, you should give only a controlled amount of praise. If they lie down but then jump right up, this is okay for now, because the down is just a down, and not a Down-Stay yet. Work these dogs for the two sessions in no distractions, and then take the two five-minute breaks on the 20-foot line, also without distractions.

The Aloof Dog—is worked as the normal-average dog and may require many corrections. No matter how long it takes, you must win out before this day's training session is allowed to end. Extremely hard corrections are needed for this dog. Work the two sessions without distractions, followed by the two five-minute breaks on the 20-foot line, also without distractions.

The Shy-afraid Dog—is worked as the normal-average, with bountiful praise everytime he lies down or is knocked down. Work this dog for two sessions without distractions, followed by the two five-minute breaks on the long line, also without distractions.

The Fear-biter,
The Aggressive Dog—These dogs should once again be staked out with the 12-foot line, as was described on the first day of heeling for them. It is very important that you do not attempt what follows without first taking this precaution. It is quite certain that at this stage of training your dog can take physical corrections from you without thinking of biting you; however, because of the newness of today's routine, the possibility exists that some dogs might make a mistake. So we will play it safe and begin with the dog staked out on the 12-foot safety line, in any case.
　　Begin heeling your dog in a counterclockwise circle around the stake or tree. Work him on a couple of stops with just automatic sits, then work him on a Sit-Stay, then a couple more automatic sits. Make a right turn, and come to a stop with the safety line taut. You and your dog should be facing away from the stake. Give a STAY command and leave, only going two feet from him, then turning and facing him. At this point your dog should not be able to reach you or make physical contact with you. He should be restrained by the safety line. Give your dog the DOWN command, Dream, DOWN, as you face him from two feet away, bowing forward slightly. If your dog lies down, verbally praise him and move off with a new HEEL command, continuing to walk around the

DOWN CORRECTION
WITH SAFETY LINE
FOR AGGRESSIVE DOG

stake in a counterclockwise circle. If, after four seconds, he does not lie down, immediately correct in the following manner: with both hands together, tightly holding the leash, slowly move toward the dog to create slack in the leash. Then silently jerk in the downward direction, to your left side, with one powerful thrust. This correction should be so forceful that it immediately compels your dog to lie down. If, for any reason, he is still not lying down, repeat the command and, after four seconds, provide a new correction. If necessary, continue alternating correction with command until you finally win out. No matter how many corrections it takes, once he is down, verbally praise him and move on with a new HEEL command, continuing to walk around the stake in a counterclockwise circle.

If your dog should misjudge your intentions and attempt to bite you as you are correcting him for the down, he will be stopped by the safety line after moving an inch or two. If your dog does attempt to bite you, move in quickly and lift him upward as you bellow NO! You will find it easy to control his body movements with the helpful opposing pull of the safety line making it impossible for the dog to reach you. After you have put him down and his aggression has ceased, tell him to SIT and STAY and, stepping back two feet, bow forward and again give the DOWN command. Repeat the procedure of correcting in this manner every time he attempts to bite you, and immediately move on to a new DOWN command and corrections. As soon as he is down, verbally praise him and

194

heel him off, continuing in a counterclockwise circle around the stake. Continue by making a couple of stops with just automatic sits; and again turning to the right, stopping, facing away from the stake, give the STAY command and leave your dog. Then turn and face him from two feet away. Give the DOWN command and if, after four seconds, he does not respond, again correct in the downward direction. If he lies down, praise him; if not, continue alternating every four seconds between correction and command until you win out. Then move off in a counterclockwise direction with a new HEEL command.

When you get four successful downs in a row, without any corrections being needed, you may end the first part of the day's training with the usual break. The break will be in the same distraction-free area, with the 20-foot line dragging. After the break, bring your dog back to the safety line and begin heeling him counterclockwise around the stake as before. After a couple of stops with just automatic sits, again come to a stop with both of you facing outside of the circle. Give the STAY command. Turn facing him, two feet away, and give the DOWN command. After four seconds, if he lies down, praise him, and move off with a new HEEL command. If he does not lie down, apply the usual hard, silent correction, praise him after he is down, and then move off with a new HEEL command. After two more successful downs you can unsnap the safety line and begin working him exactly as before, including around the circle to make it look the same to him. Continue working him as before, mixing automatic sits, Sit-Stays, and downs, for another five minutes. Then give him the usual five-minute break in the same distraction-free area, on the 20-foot line, and end this session for today. You should never again need a safety line on your dog.

THE SEVENTH DAY

The Normal-average Dog—Enter the training area with your dog. Warm him up with the usual routine of heeling, automatic sits, and an occasional stay. Then come to a stop and, as soon as he sits, bow forward slightly and give your dog the DOWN command. As soon as he lies down, praise him and move on with a new HEEL command. Needless to say, if he failed to lie down after four seconds, you would correct in the usual manner. Work your dog on a few automatic sits and then come to a stop. Give your dog the DOWN command. As soon as he is down give him an additional STAY command, which will consist of the word STAY and your open hand in front of his face. Leave him by stepping out only two steps, then turn and face him. Then immediately return to his side,

DOWN-STAY SIGNAL AND COMMAND

praise him, and move off with a new HEEL command. At the next stop leave him on a short 15-second Sit-Stay, and return, praise him, and move on with a new HEEL command. Then come to a stop and, when he sits, command, Dream, DOWN, and then, as soon as he complies, give the command word and signal STAY. Again, leave some two feet from him and turn facing him, this time for ten seconds. Return and praise.

If your dog has a tendency to sit up as you return to praise him, return slowly, and hesitate three or four seconds before praising him. This will help to keep him there as he waits for the praise. Continue working your dog on the entire heeling routine. Then come to a stop and command, Dream, DOWN, and STAY. This time walk a full six feet away before turning to face him. If he breaks at this point, by getting up, you must correct him by applying a downward horizontal jerk, together with the word NO. This should occur as he is getting up. Then, if he does not lie down, give a new command, Dream, DOWN and, once he is, add the command STAY as you show him the palm of your hand from the full six feet away. After ten seconds return to his side, praise him, and move on

DOWN-STAY 6 FEET AWAY

DOWN-STAY 2 FEET AWAY

DOWN CORRECTION FROM
6 FEET AWAY

with a new HEEL command. Vary the work for a few minutes, until you again come to a stop and do another Down-Stay from the entire six-foot length of the leash, this time for 20 seconds. Return to his side, praise him, and heel him near to where the 20-foot line is lying on the ground. Give him his usual break on the 20-foot line at this time. There will be no distractions for the work session or the breaks.

For the second training session, work all the obedience commands, including the Down-Stays, so that there is no predictable pattern to them. Vary the length of time of the Down-Stays, from 15 to 30 seconds, for this entire session. Remember that although your Down-Stays are only 30-seconds maximum at this point, your Sit-Stays are still a-minute-and-a-half maximum.

Occasionally, after learning the DOWN command, a dog will start going down by himself, for example on a Sit-Stay. This usually means that you are doing too many downs or giving the DOWN command too often to your dog. If this should occur with your dog, the first and best correction would be to prevent it from happening at all by doing very few downs for a while; this shows him that he is not going to be asked to lie down very frequently, but only occasionally. The other correction takes place when he is on a Sit-Stay and decides to lie down without command. You must be watching closely as he starts to move toward the ground. Take up the slack in the leash, holding it in your left hand, level with your chest. With an upward swing, catch the leash in the palm of your right hand and exert an upward tension, making it difficult for your dog to lie down. Then repeat the commands Dream, SIT and STAY, showing him the palm of your hand. If your dog should make it to the down position before you can exert an upward tension on the leash, you must return to him, lift him up by the collar (not the leash) back into the sit position, repeat the commands Dream, SIT and Dream, STAY again, and leave for a second time. It is, of course, preferable to catch him before he lies down. Never jerk your dog if he starts to lie down by himself. This will just *make* him lie down. Vary the work and, after 15 minutes, end the session with the usual five-minute break. Both work sessions and breaks should have no distractions present.

The Overfriendly Dog,
The High-strung Dog—Work these dogs as the normal-average. They should be built up very gradually on the Down-Stays.

The Aloof Dog—is worked as the normal-average, remembering to correct very hard if he renews any of his resistance.

UPWARD TENSION
WHEN DOG TRIES TO
LIE DOWN FROM
SIT-STAY

LIFTING UP BY THE
COLLAR TO CORRECT
DOWNING ON A SIT-STAY

199

The Shy-afraid Dog—is worked as the normal-average dog. This dog has a tendency to over-down, which may take the form of downing while on a Sit-Stay or turning an automatic sit into an automatic down. The previous remedies apply here; such as working very few downs, demonstrating to the dog that the down command will not be used frequently. As he realizes this, his confidence will return and he will remain sitting up. If, while on a Sit-Stay, he attempts to lie down by himself, exert the upward tension on the leash with your right hand, thereby preventing him from doing so. While holding him up, just verbally praising him very softly— GOOD BOY, JUST RELAX—will help to give him confidence and keep him up. If your dog develops an automatic down each time you stop, the way to work him out of this problem is, first, to do very few, or no, downs for a while, then make a few stops of a half-second duration. These stops will be so short that he barely has time to sit and you are off again. This quick routine will build up his confidence, as well as make it impossible for him to lie down.

The Fear-biter,
The Aggressive Dog—These dogs should be worked as the normal-average. Over-downing, particularly by the fear-biter, should be handled as previously described.

THE RECALL

Everyone wants his dog to come to him when called. There are two primary ways to help ensure that your dog will come. First, you must convince your dog that you can always make him come when you call him. Then, you must make coming to you an extremely pleasant thing for your dog by praising him lavishly each time he does so. This means that calling your dog to you to reprimand him or punish him for something he has done just then, or previously, is a definite mistake. We cannot emphasize this enough: if your dog learns that coming to you is going to mean punishment for him, then he is not going to be thrilled with the prospect of coming to you. Remember the way dogs learn. Those experiences that bring unpleasant results are discontinued; those that bring pleasant results are continued. Make sure your dog has a pleasant association in mind when you call him.

THE FIRST DAY

The Normal-average Dog—Enter the training area with your dog on

THE RECALL

leash and begin working him on the entire obedience routine in a distraction-free area. The routine should consist of the entire heeling procedure, including all appropriate turns and stops, an occasional Sit-Stay, and an occasional Down-Stay. After some three or four minutes, when your dog is warmed up and working well, leave him on a Sit-Stay and, as usual, stand facing him from the six-foot length of the leash. You should now call your dog to come to you, in the following manner: as you are standing facing your dog, without moving, transfer the leash to your left hand. With your right hand reach out toward your dog, and slowly draw your hand back to your chest as you give the verbal command, Dream, COME. The emphasis should be on the command word COME.

Your dog will have only one of two reactions to this new command. The first and most desirable reaction will be that he comes to you. Without pulling on the leash, take it up, hand over hand and, as he comes close to you, give the command SIT. As soon as he sits in front of you, quickly move to the heel position and praise him. Notice that he was not praised just for coming to you, but only after he came and then sat. The recall is such a vital command, that it is important for us to add the sit as an ending to the recall command. Your dog will strive to give you more

201

than just a recall, and will concentrate not only on the recall but also on the sit that follows. His concentrating on the sit will help him to do a better recall.

His second reaction will be that he does not come, but remains either sitting or standing just looking at you. If this is the case with your dog, then simply show him that you can make him come by reeling him in hand over hand and, as he draws close to you, give the command SIT. As soon as he is sitting, smoothly step to the heel position at his side and praise him.

Although we want your dog to sit in front of you after he comes to you, this is one time when *you must not correct him* if he does not sit or refuses your SIT command as he comes close to you. If coming to you means that he is going to get jerked with a correction, then, in his mind, coming to you will be considered an unpleasant thing. Therefore, once your dog is in front of you, if he refuses your SIT command, push his rear end and place him on a sit. Then lavishly praise him, thus making this a pleasant experience for him.

Begin working your dog again. Come to a stop and leave him on a Down-Stay. After a minute, return to him, take up the leash, and praise him. Continue heeling your dog, and do a Sit-Stay where you just return to him and praise him. On your next stop, leave him on a Sit-Stay and, after ten seconds, call him to you. Remember, the emphasis is on the command word COME. The command is given with the same emphasis as is given on all other commands, such as Dream, DOWN; Dream, STAY; etc. Once you sit him in front of you, move to the heel position at his side and praise him, moving off with a new HEEL command.

It is important to note at this time that no recalls will be made for now from the down position, but will only be done while your dog is on the Sit-Stay. The reason you will not call your dog to you from a Down-Stay at this time is that we want the Down-Stay to become very steady in your dog's mind. To help make it so, we will show your dog that he will not be asked to break the Down-Stay to come to you from this position. For now, you will only do recalls from a Sit-Stay.

Continue working your dog on the entire routine of heeling, Sit-Stays, Down-Stays, and recalls from the Sit-Stay for the remainder of this first 15-minute training session. Remember, just as with the down, recalls should not be repeated over and over, but the work should always be varied so your dog will not be able to anticipate any predictable pattern in your routine. Teaching a dog the recall is teaching him to break the stay. If the recall is overdone, then his reliability on the stay will be adversely affected. Always give your dog a varied work routine.

RECALL COMMAND AND
HAND SIGNAL

REELING IN, HAND
OVER HAND

SITTING IN FRONT OF YOU
AFTER RECALL

Give your dog a five-minute break on the 20-foot line, with distractions present. At the end of the break, stand on the clothesline he is dragging and call him to you the same way as before, Dream, COME. Whether he comes or you reel him in, once he is sitting in front of you, move to the heel position and praise him lavishly. With one quick motion, snap on the leash, snap off the clothesline, and begin working your dog on the entire obedience routine, varying the work between Sit-Stays, Down-Stays, and recalls. At the end of this work period, another five-minute break on the 20-foot line will end the session for this day. It is vitally important that, once the training session is over, neither you nor anyone else should ever call the dog unless you are in the position to reel him in, thereby enforcing your command. The misuse of this command would be counterproductive and actually tend to undo the day's training.

The Overfriendly Dog,
The High-strung Dog—These dogs should be worked as the normal-average, also increasing the Down-Stay to a full minute and varying the work among Sit-Stays, Down-Stays, and recalls. These dogs will need a controlled amount of praise lest they take advantage of you and jump all over you. This may mean that, once your dog is sitting in front of you, your praise will be verbal only, to keep things better under control. Gradually, as your dog can accept more praise, you will be able to increase it.

If these dogs are too excitable once they reach you, and jump exuberantly before you can give them the SIT command, try giving the SIT command while they are still approaching you and a few feet away. This will start them concentrating on sitting, rather than jumping, once they have arrived in front of you. If they attempt to run right past you, maintain close control on the leash, exerting a slight tension, and steer them directly in front of you. There you should then command them to SIT, with your own body maintaining a very still and erect posture. *Remember, never correct your dog for not sitting on the recall.* Place him, if necessary. Your dog is being praised for coming to you, which he already has done. The sit is to finalize and make his recall even more secure.

Work your dog for the usual two 15-minute sessions, without distractions, followed by the usual two five-minute breaks on the 20-foot line, in distractions. Remember to conclude each break by calling your dog to you and then reeling him in on the long line.

The Aloof Dog—should be worked as the normal-average. You most likely will have to reel in this dog for a while, since he generally is not interested in complying with your wishes. Increase the Down-Stays to a full minute, varying the work routine among Sit-Stays, Down-Stays, and recalls.

Work the two 15-minute sessions, without distractions. Give the five-minute breaks on the 20-foot line, in distractions, remembering to end each break with a recall.

The Shy-afraid Dog—should be worked as the normal-average, with the exception that, when you give the recall command, you should bend low and praise your dog softly as he moves toward you. You should bend low whether you have to reel him in or he comes by himself. As he draws near to you, stand up straight and give the command, SIT. Bending low will make you less imposing and will tend to make your dog come to you more freely. Standing up, once he is near, will have the opposite effect and make him sit. Remember, if these dogs have been called and then reprimanded in the past, you will have to overcome their fear of coming to you by your proper handling and by consistency in working the recall as described above. These dogs should always be lavishly praised after the recall.

Work your dog for two 15-minute sessions, without distractions, followed by two five-minute breaks on the 20-foot line, in distractions. End each break by doing a recall on the long line.

The Fear-biter,
The Aggressive Dog—These dogs should be worked as the normal-average, with Down-Stays, Sit-Stays, and recalls. When giving the recall command, you should praise these dogs as they walk toward you. Then give the SIT command and, whether you have to place them or they sit by themselves, they should be lavishly praised once you have returned to heel position.

Work these dogs for two 15-minute sessions, without distractions, followed by two five-minute breaks on the 20-foot line, in distractions. Finish the breaks by doing a final recall on the long line.

THE SECOND DAY

The Normal-average Dog,
The Overfriendly Dog,
The High-strung Dog,
The Aloof Dog,

The Shy-afraid Dog,
The Fear-biter,
The Aggressive Dog—All the dogs should be worked just as they were on the first day of the recall. This means no distractions for the work sessions. Today you should increase the Down-Stays to a minute and a half.

THE THIRD DAY

The Normal-average Dog,
The Overfriendly Dog,
The High-strung Dog,
The Aloof Dog,
The Shy-afraid Dog,
The Fear-biter,
The Aggressive Dog—Work all the dogs just as on the previous day, with the exception that you should increase the time on the Down-Stays to two minutes. Also, there should be a distraction at one end of the area throughout the training sessions and breaks.

THE FOURTH DAY

The Normal-average Dog,
The Overfriendly Dog,
The High-strung Dog,
The Aloof Dog,
The Shy-afraid Dog,
The Fear-biter,
The Aggressive Dog—All the dogs should be worked as on the previous days, the exception being that you will provide multiple distractions throughout the area on both the work sessions and the breaks. The Sit-Stays will remain at 1½ minutes and the Down-Stays will be increased to 2½ minutes.

THE FIFTH DAY

The Normal-average Dog,
The Overfriendly Dog,
The High-strung Dog,
The Aloof Dog,
The Shy-afraid Dog,
The Fear-biter,

The Aggressive Dog—All dogs should be worked as for the previous days. Increase the Down-Stays to three full minutes, in multiple distractions.

THE SIXTH DAY

The Normal-average Dog,
The Overfriendly Dog,
The High-strung Dog,
The Aloof Dog,
The Shy-afraid Dog,
The Fear-biter,
The Aggressive Dog—On this day take your dog out of the area to a shopping center or some other heavily trafficked place where many new distractions can be provided for him. Work him on all the obediences near people, cars, doors, shopping carts, stairs, and every distraction that you and he confront. Work him, praise him, and work him more, as both of you conquer each new distraction. When problems are encountered with a particular distraction, continue to work him near it and you and he will soon conquer it.

THE SEVENTH DAY

The Normal-average Dog,
The Overfriendly Dog,
The High-strung Dog,
The Aloof Dog,
The Shy-afraid Dog,
The Fear-biter,
The Agressive Dog—Enter the training area with your dog on leash. Begin heeling him and leave him on a Sit-Stay. Take a good look at him. You and he have come a long way. Remember six weeks ago when you started working him? Remember that first day, and how wild and difficult it was for both of you? Now look at him, and look at the change that you've brought about as he sits there attentively watching you. In six short weeks you've created a bond between you and your dog, a bond of respect and understanding that has increased with every passing day. You are to be congratulated, but you must also understand one thing. It is not over—it's just the beginning. You haven't finished training your dog. You've only just begun! In six short weeks you've come with him this far. How far can you both go in six weeks more, or in six months more? Dogs

207

USING SHOPPING CENTER DISTRACTIONS TO BUILD UP THE DOG'S RELIABILITY

differ from all other animals because of their great desire to please us. The authors of this book hope that you will continue to work your dog so that you both may become all that you are capable of being.

A MOMENT FOR REFLECTION!

Adult Problems

BARKING—

Barking is a perfectly natural thing for your dog to do, as his own mind justifies this action. It is the way he earns his keep. Whether or not he offers physical protection, he is still doing his job if he warns you by barking when strangers are near. The best way to quiet a barking dog when you are with him would be to let him drag his leash and correct him each time he begins to bark. The correction would be the word NO, sharply spoken, accompanied by a simultaneous jerk on the leash. As soon as he stops barking he should be praised. By constantly creating the contrast between correction and praise, your dog will soon make the choice that he considers most pleasant, and your consistency in this procedure will bring about the eventual end of his barking problem. The correction is most effective when coupled with obedience training because your dog will have an intimate familiarity with the word NO, and its full implications as regards your expectations from him. For barking problems when you leave him alone, see the section on BARKING under Puppy Problems.

BITING—

A biting dog is a severe problem. Biting is a dog's one action that cannot be tolerated, as a dog is capable of inflicting tremendous damage with his bite. Most owners are not aware of this because the slight nips and scratches that are occasionally inflicted upon them by their own dogs lull them into thinking that that is all a dog is capable of. Actually most dog owners never get to see, and are therefore not aware of, their dog's full biting potential. For example, the average two-year-old German shepherd weighing 65 pounds has a biting potential of from 400 to 700 pounds of pressure. This is equal to the force of a 400-to-700-pound punch press, which means that such a dog has the power in his jaws to break your arm easily or break any bones in your arms or legs or take a chunk the size of your fist out of any part of your head or body should he decide he wants to. Bigger dogs like St. Bernards have much more power behind their bites, and the ratings on them have exceeded 1000 pounds of pressure. Of course it is proportionately less for smaller dogs. A small dog weighing between 25 and 35 pounds would have less pressure—in such case (only) 200 to 300 pounds. But even this size dog is capable of taking a finger cleanly off with one bite if he wants to.

Without trying to scare you, the authors want everyone to realize fully the dangers that exist with biting dogs. Most biting problems are caused by dogs being hit, as an ineffective means of housebreaking, or put in some situation where they are teased. For instance, we know of a very sweet Great Dane puppy that was left alone in his fenced yard every day for a year at the approximate time that children were coming home from school. The children amused themselves daily by throwing sticks and rocks into the yard, all of which were aimed at the dog. The children also provided agitation by yelling at and teasing the dog as they went by. After a year of such treatment this dog turned aggressive and tried to attack any child that got anywhere near it. What had happened was that this particular dog had been taught and conditioned to believe that the little people, namely children, existed only to torture and torment him. He was only responding to what he had learned.

The rectifying of this negative experience took much time and expense, and the problem should never have been allowed to develop. It is an example of a good dog turned into a biter through no fault of his own. Although the problem was overcome by positive training, it would have been much kinder to the dog never to have allowed such unjustifiable agitation to occur. What your dog becomes is shaped very early in his puppy stages. Basically, when a dog is hit he will respond by biting. The greatest single cause of dogs' biting is *not* poor temperament, but mistreatment by misinformed owners that turns their lovable pets into defensive and aggressive potential threats to everyone.

When dealing with dogs, keep in mind one important rule; NEVER, NEVER HIT YOUR DOG. With puppies, check the chapters pertaining to them, thereby avoiding biting problems before they occur. If you already have a problem, immediately stop hitting your dog and begin to follow the obedience routine in this book as it applies to the fear-biter and the aggressive dog.

CAR CHASING—

All dogs are natural hunters and so have a tendency to chase moving objects. If the object is big, or especially noisy or noticeable, that makes the chase even more attractive. This is a case, however, where just pleasant repetition (which, in the dog's mind, is good and something to be continued) creates a habit-forming problem. Chasing cars is one of the most dangerous habits any dog can get into; it must be stopped by the most drastic measures possible, since the dog's life is in danger.

If your puppy shows signs that he would like to chase cars, give him firm leash corrections accompanied by the word NO, and praise him as he steps back. Continue this consistently for a few days. By providing a negative experience for him via the leash correction every time he attempts to indulge his pleasure in car chasing, you will be transforming the heretofore pleasurable pursuit into an unpleasant experience that he will only wish to discontinue.

If you have an older dog who is already a confirmed car chaser, drastic corrections are in order. Spend a few days or a week letting your dog drag around three or four feet of clothesline attached to his collar. In this way he will become thoroughly accustomed to the feel of the slight weight of the line dragging. Don't let a chewing dog prevent you from doing this; put alum or Bitter Apple on the line. Then, with a metal choke collar on your dog, take him outside on a 20-foot clothesline. Don't work him on any obedience; just let him walk around dragging the line.

Wait for a car to pass. When it does, and he makes his charge for it, say nothing. Clutching the end of the line tightly, with both hands pressed against your chest, silently turn and run as fast as you can in the opposite direction. There will be a terrific, shocking impact at the moment your dog runs out of slack. When properly done, the force of the impact should lift your dog into the air and perhaps carry him four or five feet back in your direction. Whether he lands on his feet or on the ground, your reaction should be the same. Simply continue to clutch the line and, saying nothing, walk some five or six feet toward him, allowing more slack to come into the line; which prepares you for a second correction.

Many dogs, after the first correction, will stand looking at you, refusing to chase any more cars that pass by. Most dogs, however, will need at least one more correction, so just wait until a second car passes by. Your dog may figure that what never happened before happened once, but cannot happen again. He must be convinced that what happened once can and *will* happen again and again and again. Meet his second charge with another silent charge of your own in the opposite direction. After the impact again say nothing. Walk toward your dog, creating slack in the line. Seventy-five percent of all car-chasing dogs will simply stand with you watching the cars pass. The remaining 25 percent will require one or two more corrections before they join the others and stand with you watching the traffic pass. To your surprise, your dog will now be much more interested in watching you, and will take the temptation of each passing car as a reason to watch *you* more closely.

As your dog becomes more trustworthy, gradually allow him to drag the line. Then you can cut two feet off it each day until there is only a balance of two feet hanging from his neck, so long as he is still ignoring cars completely. If your dog should ever again, at any stage, successfully pursue a moving vehicle, everything you have previously accomplished will all be undone. This must not be permitted to happen, and can be accomplished by never allowing your dog to run loose without the control of a leash or line on him until he completely proves his reliability. Telling a dog to SIT and STAY, and working him near cars, will *NOT* favorably change his attitude. Only silent corrections, as described above, will make him decide for himself that chasing cars, from now on, is a very unpleasant thing to do and therefore is something to be discontinued.

CAT CHASING—

If the hunting instinct is kindled slightly when a car goes by, then it is surely kindled when a cat runs by. Some dogs are almost powerless to resist chasing an animal that is running away from them. Since it is a natural instinct for almost any dog, it will take persistence and consistency on your part to discourage your dog from indulging this irresistible compulsion.

Work your dog in the complete obedience routine outlined in the Obedience Training section of this book, utilizing cats as frequent distractions, until, finally, your dog can work very close to them. This will change his attitude towards cats, from being something to be chased to being just another distraction to be ignored.

CHEWING—

Adult chewing problems, while having the appearance of spite-work, are actually frustration and despair that occur when some dogs are left alone.

These dogs must never be reprimanded upon your return, since this is after the fact. Rather, they should be provided with favorable alternatives to destructive chewing, which will channel their frustrations into harmless outlets. Alternatives could take the form of rawhide leather chew toys that could be rubbed with raw bacon to make them extra attractive. They would be handed to your dog as you are leaving. For more specific information on chewing problems and their remedies, see the section on CHEWING under puppy problems.

CONTROL IN THE CAR—

When your dog has learned the five obedience commands as described in this book, it is then time to show him that the car is another place where he must also listen. He must learn that the car is a place where you can also enforce your commands. When your dog works well in distractions on his Sit-Stays and Down-Stays, you should start working him in the car. Work him on a 15-foot clothesline, in the car, with the car parked in your driveway. Begin with him holding a Sit-Stay in the back seat, with the doors open. Make corrections as needed, with the clothesline. These should consist of the usual quick jerk-and-release movement as used on the Sit-Stay with the six-foot leash. Progress to the point where the dog will hold a Sit-Stay or a Down-Stay as you get into the front seat, with the doors open and closed. Then work him with the motor running but the car still parked in the driveway, with you outside the car. Then progress to having a helper drive the car back and forth in the driveway, with you on the passenger side and your dog working for you in the back. The next step will be with you and him in the car alone, with the motor running but the car stationary. Then work him with you driving the car back and forth in the driveway and the long line still attached to him. Finally, drive in the street with regular traffic, and the line still on. This line will then be progressively shortened as his reliability increases. Although control in a moving car will not be as perfect as it is in other areas, your dog will have respect for your ability to correct in this situation, whereas he never did before.

No dog, large or small, should ever be allowed to ride in the front seat of a car at any time. Your dog should be severely reprimanded anytime he attempts to jump into the front seat. Should his attempt be successful, you must physically throw him back to where he belongs as you bellow a very loud NO! As soon as he is again in the rear seat of the car, you should praise him, GOOD BOY.

Many dogs have other car-related problems. Many dogs are terrified at the prospect of a ride in the car and their owners can't understand why. They can't understand why their dogs don't like going for extended rides with the windows closed in winter, or closed in summer because the air conditioner is on. These people don't realize that their dogs, with their supersensitive noses, are practically suffocating from exhaust fumes. Compounding the problem may be the fact that the dog may have been fed just before the trip, making it certain that he will be nauseous throughout the trip.

Whether it is a freezing-cold day in the middle of the winter, or a hot day in the summer with your air conditioner on, and no matter how comfortable *you* feel, your dog needs plenty of fresh air. This means that he needs a window partially open, at least three or four inches, somewhere near him. For safety's sake, windows should never be completely open. Mufflers and exhaust systems should be checked for leaks that would add greatly to the dog's discomfort. Dogs should have nothing to eat at least two hours before a car ride. If your dog only goes for car rides when you take him to the vet, or for other, to him, equally unpleasant excursions, then he will not be delighted with the prospect of a car ride. Just as, likewise, if he gets sick in the car, he will not want to repeat the experience.

Pleasant associations must begin to be made concerning the car and the places to which it takes your dog. Short rides to a park or other happy place will change his attitude to a more favorable one concerning the car. Short rides that don't allow him time to get sick will let him discover that being in the car doesn't make him sick. These suggestions, coupled with a good obedience program where you also work him in the car, will solve most any dog's car problems.

DOG FIGHTING—

is very dangerous and a tough problem to stop. Certain breeds are more prone to this mania than others. Dog fighters are usually cultivated when, at an early age, they are attacked by other dogs. Once the fighting instinct is kindled, it becomes a permanent part of the dog's personality and is very difficult to eradicate.

A dog that is a confirmed fighter represents an extreme physical danger to his owner, people, and other dogs. The habit must be stopped early and not given a chance to grow. Fighting dogs should never be given the opportunity to make physical contact with other dogs. They should be worked in the obedience routine, concentrating on using other

DOGFIGHTING CAN BE A SEVERE HANDICAP WHEN YOU LEAST EXPECT IT.

dogs as distractions for them, until they can be worked near other dogs and their attitude toward the others favorably improves. Since dog fighting is an extremely dangerous problem, the corrections given your dog should be very severe.

GROWLING—

There is a saying that if a dog growls at you on Monday he will be biting you by Friday. What this really means is that growling leads to nipping, and then to biting. A growling dog is warning you that he doesn't like what you are doing and, if you continue, he is going to bite you. If your dog is growling, it must be stopped before it progresses. The way to stop it is to give this dog specific hard corrections, which consist of a jerk and release on the leash, everytime he growls, and begin working him as described in the obedience section of this book. Growling must never be tolerated, and must always be corrected firmly. Growling dogs should never be hit.

JUMPING—

Dogs can't understand why, when their owners come home, they can jump on *them* and be praised for it, but get scolded and yelled at and hit for doing the same thing to strangers. Big dogs, or dogs with wet, muddy

216

feet, present an extremely unpleasant situation, and a big jumping dog can seriously injure the face of an infant. Striking your dog with a knee lift into his chest may make your dog stop jumping on you, but it won't take him long to find out that your guests are not aware of this technique and, in the case of children and old people, unable to execute it. Specific leash corrections, every time your dog attempts to jump on anyone, is the proper way to change your dog's attitude, making him realize that jumping up is no longer going to be fun. With him dragging ten feet of clothesline when company is expected, severely correct him every time he attempts to jump on anyone, and praise him each time he stops. Consistent repetition will win out for you and solve your jumping problem. Remember, you can't reprimand him one day for jumping on your guests and then praise him the next for jumping on you. Consistency is most needed by your dog so that he will clearly learn, without confusion, what is expected of him.

MOUNTING—

Mounting is an obedience problem and not a medical problem. The answer to a dog's mounting is not hormone injections or castration, although some vets will advise them. Other means are effective and much more practical. The way to stop a dog from mounting people is with a couple of extremely hard leash corrections and an obedience program as described in the obedience section of this book. There is no need for surgical operations or hormone shots of any kind.

RUNNING AWAY—

It is typical for some dogs to sneak past as you open the door, and to escape out into the street. These dogs take the open door as a green light to visit the neighbors and buzz the neighborhood. No matter how many times your dog has successfully run out through the door, and no matter how old he is, you can, in approximately one minute, stop him from running out the door. To do this you will need a choke collar with 15 feet of clothesline attached. Take your dog out of the room and have your helper prop the door so that it remains open. Re-enter the room with your dog, tightly clutching the line to your chest. Glance at your watch, take note of the time, and approach the door with your dog, ignoring him and his actions completely. As he starts running towards the door, silently make an about-turn and start running in the opposite direction. The impact should be timed to occur as the dog passes a few inches through the doorway. Immediately after the correction, still saying nothing to your dog, walk a few steps toward him, allowing slack to come into the line in case he attempts another charge out the door. If he does so, your reaction will be the same—silently turn and forcefully run in the opposite direction.

Most dogs will learn with one or two corrections; occasionally a dog will take three. No matter how many corrections a dog needs, your job is to provide them exactly as described above. If you do as instructed, you will soon see your dog standing at the threshold, looking out the open door, and looking back at you, as he refuses to go through the open door. Now look at your watch and you will notice that, just as we promised you, less than one minute has elapsed. The best way to teach a dog not to run out of an open doorway, is NOT to make him sit and stay by the door, but to let him, when he is not under command, decide for himself that going through it alone is an unpleasant thing for him to do. As this positive conditioning is repeated, his attitude will change and going through an open door will become something that he will definitely choose to discontinue.

SPAYING THE FEMALE—

The authors' advice to people about spaying their female dog can be summed up in one word—DON'T. There are two logical reasons for spaying a female dog. The first one is if she is one of the few dogs who in her "heat" period is especially messy, causing destruction to rugs and furniture. The only other possible reason is if she is in constant contact with male dogs, as, for example, living with a male dog in her own family. There is no other justifiable reason to take the extreme risk of this major surgery for any dog. Spaying your female will not calm her down, make her friendly, make her obedient, or cure any other obedience-related problems. Once again, since the risks far outweigh any possibility of benefits, the authors reiterate—DON'T.

SPITEFUL PIDDLING—

appears to be revenge on the dog's part for being left alone. He seems to be saying that he is going to get even with you for leaving him alone, and so is going to "make" in the house. Although this appears to be the case, it most often is not. In the rare instances where this is so, a good obedience program will make him respect you and effeectively will solve the problem. Most dogs with this problem, however, are not doing it for revenge but from fear that you will not return, and the secondary fear that you will

YOUR "SWEET PUPPY" MAY LOOK LIKE "TROUBLE" TO OTHER PEOPLE...

return and reprimand them. Since these dogs' mistakes occur at the same times as the spiteful dogs' mistakes, they are also often mistaken for spite-work. To cure the problem, study the housebreaking schedule in this book, leaving him for short periods of time. Upon your return, praise him and take him out immediately. Never attempt to punish the dog in any way for transgressions that he committed hourss before when you were not there.

THE MAILMAN—

It seems to be a strong conviction with many dogs that they should not like the mailman. No matter what it is that causes the dog's reaction—be it the uniform or the seeming taking something away from the house, though in reality he is leaving something—your dog's reaction with aggression, in fact anything more than a warning bark, should not be tolerated. The answer to the problem lies within the pages of the Obedience Training section in this book. As you work on obedience, and as he improves, the mailman will become just another distraction for your well-trained dog to ignore as his attention remains focused upon you above all else.